The Whole Slide

By
Ivor Vernon Smith

@ventura
eBooks

Published By @ventura eBooks

www.aventuraebooks.com

This Edition Paperback – July 2018

Copyright © Ivor Vernon Smith 2018

The Author asserts the moral right to be identified as the author of the poems contained in this work.

This anthology is entirely a work of fiction. Names, characters, businesses, places, events and incidents are either the products of the author's imagination or used in a fictitious manner. Any resemblance to actual persons, living or dead, or actual events is purely coincidental.

All rights reserved. No part of this publication may be reproduced, stored in a retrieval system, or transmitted, in any form or by any means, electronic, mechanical, photocopying, recording or otherwise, without the prior permission of the publishers.

The book is sold subject to the condition that it shall not, by way of trade or otherwise, be lent, re-sold, hired out or otherwise circulated without the publisher's prior consent in any form of binding or cover other than that in which it is published and without a similar condition including this condition being imposed on the subsequent purchaser.

Book, cover design and production by @ventura eBooks

Kindle ISBN: **978-1-909087-94-1**
Paperback ISBN: **978-1-717922-66-3**

Dedication

To Shirley

Acknowledgements

For my dear late wife Shirley
for allowing me to nurture my passion
and for originally committing my poems
to the digital world,
she would have been so proud to see them published.
Also, thanks to Keith, Sylvana,
Tracey Matthew and Peter
for their interest, help and encouragement

Preface

At the tender age of ten I recited 'The Charge of the Light Brigade' to the school and for the first time realised that it wasn't just anger or joy that revealed the emotions. There, in front of an audience, I was able to express myself with *'Flashed all their sabres bare, flashed as they turned in air'*, without being driven in any way.

So, childhood moments like these certainly affected me for the rest of my life. I didn't start writing poetry until I was thirty-seven, but what had built up in the sub-conscious during that time came to the fore one night in October 1973. I soon realised that whatever problems I had were diminished every time I wrote a poem. Since then I have written many poems and although the problems didn't vanish, it certainly became a temporary escape.

I have always thought that the best poetry is never written, so sometimes I would get out of bed to write, for I knew it would be gone in the morning. Writing verse is 90% inspirational and unlike most prose, one does receive an instant "reward".

Reading and understanding verse is one of the most subjective things in literature but no matter how obscure the meaning might be, if you read well between the lines, a different impression can be found. So, whatever the style, think of it as a painting with words.

Ivor Vernon Smith

Introduction

The date is 22nd October 1973 – 11.00 pm. I was about to go to bed when I thought, let's write a poem instead! So, I burnt the midnight oil, wrote half the poem and completed the other half at work the following day. Apart from a few attempts at prose I had never written any form of literature before but here I am forty-five years later having written approximately eighteen hundred poems.

However, I still find myself asking the same question – what is poetry? Is it just putting the right words in the right order? Are the bricks just the words, with the mortar the meaning, which if it's not properly mixed, the whole lot collapses? Certainly, one must read a great deal between the lines, no matter how much metaphor and obscurity distorts the understanding.

Modern verse is often criticised for not having enough sentiment, but it can be equally argued that much 19th century poetry is guilty of the converse. What is most important is how much meaning and depth can be concentrated into the minimum amount of lines.

When writing the following poems, I tried to avoid the dreaded clichés and platitudes which result in doggerel. Nevertheless, poetry is such a subjective form of literature the bone can be licked clean to the marrow but will always be impossible to suit all tastes.

'***Brighton Shades***' may offend some people with the imagery, but being brought up there, this is just my opinion. With '***London Eyes***' I needed to write many more verses to describe the complete city and lost myself a little in the enormity of the task. '***Old Rupert***' is about a real character who unfortunately overtaxed his brain and became deranged. '***Jessie White***' is a fictitious prostitute, and there were many other characters like this.

It has been said that prose is 90% perspiration and 10% inspiration, whereas poetry is 10% perspiration and 90% inspiration. Whether this is strictly true, they are simply different forms of literature with poetry's rhyme and meter hopefully enhancing the subject, but never to the detriment of the meaning. I think the following couplet should always apply:

'Never commit the literary crime,

Forsaking the meaning for the rhyme'

I wrote that many years ago and have tried to adhere to it – sometimes unsuccessfully.

This is where I think modern verse has the edge on nineteenth century work having far more freedom. Free verse is far less inhibited with less rhyme and less meter. Just so long as the freedom one chooses the result can only be read or recited as poetry. Here is a verse from the poem ***'Van Gogh'*** which I hope illustrates this:

Fierce strokes that flourished on a clear noon

Each thrust reflecting coordination

Unequalled by any other touch or sight,

A soul at peace with the scene

At war with its own repressions

Gulping greedily on the land's breath.

When I first wrote poetry, it seemed to me that there were so many restrictions regarding meter, I.e.: Iambic pentameter with its many variations, the arrangement of syllables – accented or unaccented and when I came to write sonnets with their fourteen lines of ten syllables tied up with rhyming

Systems, it all seemed too much of a brain cane. So, I thought (as no doubt many others have) let's write twentieth century verse with just a hint of the nineteenth century, hopefully finding the happy medium. ***'I Want to Be a Computer Dad'*** has an Orwellian theme, with the father emerging from the 'deep freeze' which the technology from the next generation had made possible at the expense of their emotions. Here is the last verse:

When you awake to a time and place

With the hour of disease long denied

And you gaze deep into my digital face

Will you see where the tear-wells are dried?

It has been said many times that life is morbid enough without having to write about it, but this is acceptable whether it is sad or comical, so long as there is some truth along the way. Something like this perhaps:

THE LAST WORD

There are those who save

There are those who spend

There are those who borrow

There are those who lend

But the ones with any sense at all

Are those who spend and leave sod all,

Or lie content without regret

Buried, smiling, deep in debt.

I have endeavoured to include as much variety as possible in this book of poems and trust the subjects and style are of sufficient interest. We all have a different way of reading with different expectations, but one thing we should all have in common when reading verse, according to Stephen Fry in his "***Ode Less Travelled***", is that it can never be read too slowly.

Table of Contents

Dedication

Acknowledgements

Preface

Introduction

Table of Contents

PART I – Short Poems
- TRIANGLED 1
- TRAIN OF THOUGHT 2
- THE LONELY DREAM 4
- THE LAST WORD 5
- CHRISTOPHER JOHN 6
- TRAITORS' FATE 7
- THE WAITING ROCK 8
- PHANTOM 9
- ON PROGRESS 10
- HAMMER OF SILENCE 11
- BECAUSE 12
- THE PUREST EVIL 13
- I BREATHE 14
- VEHICLE OF WORDS 15
- JUST FOR YOU 16
- NARCISSUS HILL 17
- PINHEAD 18
- SAFETY CURTAIN 19
- LEMON SWEET 20
- VERTIGO TOWER 21
- UNSUNG GENES 22
- TARGETS 23
- HARSH COMFORT 24
- HOW SOON THE LIGHT 25
- TO SHIRLEY 26
- A WEAKENING STRENGTH 27
- DINING WITH THE GODS 28
- FORTY SHADES 29
- WHERE GOES LOVE 30
- LATE MOVE 32
- MISSING PIECE 33

CARE	34
QUICK, QUICK, SLOW	35
AVANT GARDE	36
THE MOVING WIRE	37
WASTE – BLINDNESS	38
SENTENCED TO JOY	39
THE LEARNING	40
A THORN DEFILED	41
A DUBIOUS TREASURE	42
A DEATH BEFORE DYING	43
RUMBA NIGHTS	44
UNQUIET THOUGHTS	45
NOVELTY'S DISCIPLINE	46
FARMER FOP AND URCHIN	47
LET US CONTINUE TO LIE	48
SURREALIST DAY	49
CYCLING	50
OLD IDEALS	51
BETWEEN PROGRAMMES	52
TRICKS	53
WE THE BRITISH	54
RIDERS	55
THE DARK SHORE	57
MR. BIG	58
JUDGE AND JURY	59
BEAT THE RETREAT	60
LOST LOVE	61
THE SCHEME OF THINGS	62
FACADE	64
HERITAGE OF DUST	65
THE LAST BOMB	66
MIRROR, MIRROR	67
HELL'S GATHERING STORM	68
FREUD	70
THE QUIET PLACE	72
A Marriage Sonnet	72
DRY INHIBITION	73
LISTENING	74
THERE WAS A TIME	75
BRIGHTON SHADES	76
VAN GOGH	78
SIEGE	80
CHILD OF MAY	81

THE TIGHT-ROPE WALKER	83
FAREWELL	84
I WANT TO BE A COMPUTER DAD	85
THE DARK SHEET	86
WATERLOO BRIDGE	87
CATS!	88
A MEMORY'S BONDAGE	89
NONSENSE	91
A 1970'S APPETITE	92
A CANTERBURY DREAM	93
PRIDE	95
ANOREXIA NERVOSA	96
OUR ALEX	97

PART II – Sonnets

PAUPER KING	101
DREGS	102
GOLFER'S EYE	103
BELLS OF WAR	104
SONNET TO DIANA	105
FORGOTTEN LIMBO	106
Sonnet to my son's coma	106
SONNET TO SHIRLEY	107
UPON THIS APRIL DAY	108
A Wedding Sonnet	108
WIMBLEDON ECHOES	109

PART III – Longer Poems

THE GIRL IN THE WOODS	113
ODE TO THE SELF-EMPLOYED	117
OLD RUPERT	119
STROLLED IN SILENT MISTS OF GREY	121
NAKED RHYTHM	122
BOLERO	123
SUMMER LEGS	124
SCORING	125
FURORE	126
TRUST	127
THE YELLOW SEA	128
THE BALLAD OF THE GREY & BLUE	130
REASON'S RHYME	133
A COMPUTER WEPT	134
ULTRA SENSITIVITY	135
BROOKLYN BRIDGE	136

APPRECIATION	137
THE CAVE	138
THE LONGEST DREAM –	139
On My Father's Death	139
BOGGED BLIND IN BULL	141
ONE MAN BAND	142
THAT'S ALL	143
THE BALLAD OF JESSIE WHITE	144
THE SCRIBE	149
ONE BACKWARD GLANCE	150
JUST A THOUGHT	151
JANUARY'S BRIDE	152
FOOLS ELEGY	153
GEOMETRICALLY OPPOSED	154
DEPRESSION'S DUST	155
REBELLION	156
COULD I WITHIN A TRAUMA WRITE	157
AUTOPILOT	159
WINTER 'GAINST MY CHEEK HAS BRUSHED	160
WHAT'S HER NAME?	161
THERE'S SIMILE AND METAPHOR	163
GUTTER	164
WHEN	165
THE PARTNER	166
THE FINGER ON THE TRIGGER	168
LISTEN, MY LOVE	169
TRADITION	170
AN ANT IN THE WILDERNESS	171
EN PASSANT	172
Be it Heaven or Hell - **all is in passing.**	172
FOOLS IN THE SUN	174
FIGHT!	175
INSOMNIA DESPERANDUM	176
BEGGAR	177
A MOMENT HELD	178
IN STARK SUBSIDENCE	180
APOLOGY	182
THE STUBBORN DAY	183
IVY–CLAD TRADITION	184
SECOND GENERATION	186
THE GIRLS OF AUTUMN	190
SUSPICION'S COVER	193
SYRUP	194

ONE EDGED SWORD	195
LONDON EYES	197
YOU ALONE HAVE HEARD	204
FROZEN CHEER	205
OLD TWISTER	206
LINE OF DISTINCTION	207
OUR RHYME	209
DRUNK'S ELEGY	210
SLEDGEHAMMER BLUES	211
BOOMERANG	212
SUMMER'S TORTURE	213
IF TEARS MUST FALL	214
ON MALTA	215
ON DREAMS	216
ON SICKNESS	217
PARANOIDEXPERTITIS	218
PERHAPS IT'S JUST ME	219
QUICK QUICK SLOW	220
DISSERVICE	221
A CHOICE?	222
NEVER	223
THE CUT	224
A PAWN GOES FORTH	225
DO I AWAKE?	226
PRECOCIOUS DAWN	227
AIR-SICK	228
TUMBRILS ARE RUMBLING	229
HEADS OR TAILS?	230
SPARK	231
DARK FORM OR ESSENCE	232
A CHILD'S NIGHT OUT	233
VESUVIUS DAY	234
NARROW PRAYER	235
IF THERE IS A POINT	236
AGNOSTIC EYE	237
GAMES	240
THE HAUNTER OF MY DARKEST SLEEP	241
NEGLECT	242
CHINESE WHISPERS	244
MARRIED BLISS?	245
THE DAY OF THE SALESMAN	246
ON FRIENDSHIP	248
THE UNFINISHED SUPPER	249

WEDDING SPEECH 251
BEING 253
LOGICAL BOLLOCKS 255
MIND OF DESPAIR 257
BUFFER 259
THE BALLAD OF MELINDA GREY 261
MIRROR 264
EL MONTGO 265
MINOR KEY 267
INDECISION 268
SLANG 269
I TOUCHED THE SADNESS THERE 270
SCARLET GREY 271
A DEEPER AUTHORITY 272
IMPASSE 273
WHAT DOES IT MATTER 274
NOWHERE 276
LOVE'S HABIT LOST 277
SCRUFFS 279

About the Author

PART I – Short Poems

TRIANGLED

Love cornered
Tied through design
Purposely tangled
Precise in firm comfort
With joys measured area.
The bait of mildness timelessly dangled
Swings in caution's caressing breeze
Avoiding temptation's magnetic noose
Choking affection, geometrically strangled,
Yet through restriction, finely pointed,
Comes love-born feelings' definition
Be it acute or obtusely angled
Fits neat and strong in perfection's corner
Isosceles pair in adoration
Of nature's cherished jewel, dream spangled,
Bonding forever a blessing-filled threesome,
Love, hope and reason joining as one.
See a symmetry, securely angled
Shaped in consistency level and sharp,
Like we trust our souls will ever be
Living in peace with a truth untangled.

17th November 2003

Ivor Vernon Smith

TRAIN OF THOUGHT

I board the train each pensive morn
And see a clock's unfriendly face;
My purpose is forever torn
Between the home and working place.

Doors are slamming, whistles blown'
With sleep still hung upon my eyes
I meditate how I have grown
Within this wilderness of sighs

I gaze around the muted crowd
And sense the secrets lying there,
No need for some to think aloud,
Those faces lined with stress-grown care.

To feel the meter and the rhyme
That forms the rhythm of each thought
I sit there blind and deaf to time
Regardless in what web I'm caught.

Across the points, we clatter by,
Someone coughs, those papers rustle,
My reverie – a shattered sigh;
Join the steam, milling bustle.

One station less to city rush
To meet the challenge of the day
Then blend within the homeward crush
For final insults of delay.

A lonely platform welcomes me,
A blessing waits with beauty's smile,
Depression's tunnel soon will flee
Along that last impatient mile.

It matters not how small the light
For a positive inspection,
Providing that the track's laid right
And my train knows which direction.

2003

THE LONELY DREAM

We rode the night together
This lonely dream, and I,
'cross fields of moonlit heather
To touch the passive sky.

I hung my bridle from a star
And raced the yellow cloud
That swept my yesterday afar
As through night's void we ploughed.

We held as one a sweet embrace
This lonely dream and I,
Till slowly turning from that face
With eyes that would not lie,

I groped at fading visions
With inward yearning sight,
To make the dark decisions
Ere dawn would end their flight.

With slackened rein we sped the course,
Spurred on by the wind's applause,
Till this glist'ning body spent its force
Through effects of a daily cause.

We fled the night together,
This lonely dream and I,
I led my steed to tether
And left him with a sigh.

1974

THE LAST WORD

There are those who save
There are those who spend
There are those who borrow
And there are those who lend
But the ones with any sense at all
Are those who spend and leave sod all
Or lie content without regret
Buried, smiling, deep in debt.

CHRISTOPHER JOHN

How well conceived your fine move
On the last gasp of Summer,
So much achieved in future's aim
Through that well concealed plot
Interminable in execution
Yet sweet and secure in comfort,
As nature conspired with hope
To temper expectancy's wish
Blending all life and creed
With unmeasured certainty,
Till the pain of giving is released
And all this breath is yours
For you to spread at leisure
Across the unsuspecting earth.
Now you have learnt control
From your physical domain
As you leave me well used
Glowing in agony's respite
When the careless wind howled
On that milky natal dawn,
And you were there in truth
With all the essence of being
Closer to God's secret
Than infinity could disclose,
Filled with an untapped love,
With you and I alone
Like we would never be again
A moment apart, yet as one.

2004

TRAITORS' FATE

Intelligence who or intellect why
It matters little where the blades are crossed
Or by what emphasis a meaning tossed
On unfathomed ocean or endless sky.
Bring me the motive, bring me the reason
Turn up the volume on neurons' delight
Witness old methods of winning the fight
Just is the hand that punishes treason.

Dead is the patriot shelled in the dust
Through covert intrigue a nation destroyed
Deception's baptism bearing love's cross
Caretakers of time inflated with lust
Persuading an hour to stay unemployed
Shaking the hand that recovers the loss.

2nd May 2000

THE WAITING ROCK

My mind a half built house of unmade beds,
A one-way corridor that never ends,
A pattern less tapestry's unstitched threads,
A planet where continuous night descends.
Come, hear my dirge where music once was played
Old listening ears now hear time's discord
And moral breath is hushed, whose tongue betrayed
The fresh euphoria that my eyes applaud.
How shall I lock the undefended door
That shuts upon repression's room of clues
When pleading from insular, warped floor
For all the channelled calm fair tide can choose.
Now in the shallow bowels that move success
Come see the waiting rock my spade will press.

3rd February 1999

PHANTOM

Was this the purest music of desire
Capturing an ambiance of numbed pain
To drive her octave through a tortured fire
Revengeful of an agony's last stain.
Was this one step adjacent to the grave
That felt a justice in hell's solitude
To cultivate acoustics and enslave
The nurtured voice enshrined in attitude.

No mask to hide creation's inner cry
Entwined within the labyrinths of his soul
Where pathos turned fame's spotlight all awry
And spread a pathway to a shadow role
To vanish in flair's enigmatic sigh
As gothic bells invite dusk's haunting toll.

14th March 2000

ON PROGRESS

Indistinct though subtle in the passing
The tree of progress spreads relentless boughs
Casting forgotten shadows on tired vows
That once held all promise everlasting.
We check our individual stride, stumbling
Down ambiguous avenues to depose
The power that overwhelms when hearts propose
Marooning on an unrequited humbling.
Contentment pales before conditioned needs
Ignited as a values glare distorts
An inspiration's vista set in gold
Invested from those dictatorial seeds
Wildly growing from amplified reports
Blooming where dead shares are finally sold.

13th April 2000

HAMMER OF SILENCE

If all the pieces fit
What futile aim is gained
Should they remain face- down;
The puzzle increasing
In complexity and design,
A panic of neuron's
Metaphoric haste conspires
Through a study of guessing
On the reverse side of logic
Where a blank shaped image
Holds deduction's unturned key.

Uncertainty's menu scanned
Digging into stress pie's crust
We relish a nerve sweet dessert
And complain with satisfaction
At integrity's smile
Breaking all emotion's rules
With the hammer of silence.

So we have our endless fill
Insatiable yet bloated
To turn our puzzle gut side up
Bulging shameless within the frame.

26th October 1999

BECAUSE

I write because I must
To wipe away the dust
That settles on my mind
Building cancerous rust.

Let word -wave's fever pour
To flood thoughts pensive shore
And mix a phrase to find
Truth in a tempest's roar.

Spring's tree her roots spread deep
Till sap sprung branches leap
On to the sky bound page
An author's scythe to reap.

Ignore the gain- sick lust
Resist the fame- wind's gust
Care not for fool or sage
And write because you must!

13th October 1999

THE PUREST EVIL

There's pure evil in self-pity
Surmounting passive barriers
It festers in a groaning wound
Soothed by amoral carriers.
The wielded implement hope – worn
Is thrust in artificial hands
Like an unsigned blank cheque offered
Whilst sin's cashier never understands.

There's a fortune of old sayings
Abandoned on decaying walls
Where families once held hostage
Were tied with spite that hate recalls,
And though avenged our thoughts live on
To gain the strength in comfort's aim
That revels in power's voodoo dart
Where demons win the spellbound game.

I BREATHE

I breathe, A world of heads recoil
They catch
Nothing, nor ever will,
Yet some
Remain convinced in spite
Of proof
As clear as breath itself
That air
Holds all contamination
And spreads
A plague of paranoia
Whose pulse
With manic nerve is felt
To draw
A virus-vapoured veil
Unseen
Touching time eternal
To preach
An undenying sermon
That marks an endless agony
For those
In trust's false premise locked,
Where freed
Our sphere is spun and dried.
I breathe,
My Universe inhales.

24th September 1999

VEHICLE OF WORDS

Slowly, the vehicle of words
Draws past fresh opportunity's stage
Powered by bubbling incentive
Burst and deflated
On realization's sorry road.
Thoughts axle drags and grinds
Philosophy-heavy with ideal;
Coloured syntax in expression
Forms appropriate phrasing
On discussion's mouthing journey
Oozing with articulation
To the first strains of silence
Reaching the first upward slope
As discomfort grows through uncertainty
Like dusk's early shadows.
Ideology groping for space,
Tentacles in defiance spread,
Retracting in sympathy
When all listening ceases
Till comprehension's peak is reached
Piercing fault-layered system's cloud
Where slipped opinion's downhill run
Sledges past fear's hesitant drift.
The icebound stanzas melt and flow
Down to fluidity of fair debate
Our vehicle halts, frozen in neutral,
Cliché –idling in the dark
Whispering to nothingness

11th August 1999

JUST FOR YOU

Repetitious anecdotes
Shackling strained attention
Into boredom's slavery.
Far better banal platitudes
Thickening inert silence
Drawing heavily on the obvious
Yet seeking scant reply
From an affable treasury
Where gems of tact rehearse
A patronising farce.

Vulnerable the naked ear
Word stormed in thundery air
When hearing passes on advice
That listening tends to keep.
Still comes the adage with the tale
To colour nothing on stale walls

Fresh paint upon archaic decay,
Yet still it drones, endless and flat,
Deceiving but the speakers tongue
Inspired by tolerant nod.

A comedy produced in vain
A muted audience captured whole,
A monologue of glib effect
Fires interest yearning for an end
With built in encore just for you.

27th *July 1999*

NARCISSUS HILL

High upon Narcissus hill
Magnified temptation hung,
And a cross filled mouth preached
A sinless love, a soul spun creed.
Vanity checked her vision
Added power's vast turnover
Multiplied greed's probabilities
Divided integrity's purpose
Deducted hypocrisy's expenditure
Tasted expectancy's gross profit
Swallowed vanity's golden feast
Spat out the pips of honesty
Upon the fields of promise
Understating the shallow loss
Of potential conscience.

Now in knee skinning reverence
Let us absorb sermons of desire
Exhaling the balance of dreams
Upon unsuspecting visionaries;
How to justify amoral heights
Lost in cliché-clouded corruption
When mothers of cherished eyes
Rock feverishly a death's head cradle
High beyond Narcissus hill
Guiding trust through an unseen Universe.

20th January 1998

PINHEAD

Was there ever really nothing
Before the bursting of a finite shell,
For even space in purest form
Existed subject to a magnetic matter
Drawn by a timeless void,
Where abstract element's incipient breath
Sighed at infinity's wealth
Formed a relative pause
For a pinhead universe's
Volcanic egg's eruption
Containing past, present, future
Life, death, good and evil,
Like our untapped brain waiting
For another switch activating
The part and whole of being,
A microism to absolute power
Outweighing all judgement and design
That holds futility and purpose as one
In the solid state of nothingness
When dying holds the key to life.

29th February 1998

SAFETY CURTAIN

Curtain parting silken facts
On mimicry's unquiet performance
By a raw word-scattering cast
Lit with a day fused spotlight
Unrehearsed on yesterday's back lot.
The safety curtain gently lowers
Endorsing portrayal's division,
Freshly simplified opinions bantered
With euphoric numbing judgement
Till a gin-oiled music machine
Bursts expectancy's balloon
And unmeasured time strains by.

Now comes a sotto voce prompt,
Fantasy's reality destroyed.
Who cares! We tore the script up long ago
Props malfunctioned, scenery collapsed,
Drama turned comedy, plot forgotten,
Farce without timing, tragedy - doomed.
So comes the star, distant yet close
Performing nothing yet doing the most.

A safety curtain in the dark
Self-protecting whom from what?

30th March 1998

LEMON SWEET

Squeeze dry the weeping lemon,
Replacing the two halves,
It looks the same before cutting
In body and symmetry.
So from my deceptive shell
I smile from nothing,
The colour unchanging,
An assured performance
With well intrinsic values displayed,
Knowing enough for forfeiture
Yet uncaring in my gain.

Now all moral issues fly
To a sheltering space
Defiling trust's consecration,
Spiralling in wild ascendancy
A full and lengthy fluttering,
A butterfly relativity
Bearing all strength and certainty;
And I, retaining a dried shell,
Yearn for the wasted chrysalis,
Squint through my lemon tears
Hearing sweet Utopia on a sour note.

VERTIGO TOWER

Stale wisdom daily yawning
Tolls academia's frantic bell
Pulled by study's fraying rope
In a term of Autumn ruin

Once (when youth had climbed its tower
To wallow in that spell of vertigo)
They gazed on March field's indecision
Not knowing when to spring their seed
And spread the harvest of impression's dream
Disregarding expectancy's keen scythe.

Pressure guides mounting stress and stabs
The knowledge-belching underbelly
Where deep digestion floods the heart
And holds a drowning tongue to ransom.

How scales young reason on logical heights
Watching toil's avalanche bury pleasure
When unheld ethics guess the honest lie
Judgmental of incipient growth
To draw a learning culture to its peak
Surveying all and knowing less.

So intellect in dizzy splendour,
Let not dull sweat inhibit joy
Life's curriculum hard and tender
Has endless subjects to employ.

24th February 1999

UNSUNG GENES

Reasoning baffled
Miracles born
Ego unruffled
Regardless of scorn
Biological doubt
Knowledge denied
Truth squeezing out
Compassion has dried.
Conditioned to birth
Blindly achieved
Formed nature's worth
Numbly conceived.
Genetics erupt
Lava to ash
Body corrupt
From mind's endless lash,
Cannon unfired
Blast never felt
Orders inspired
Words never spelt.
Volume of living
Turned to extremes
Takes all the giving
Shows what it seems.

13th April 1999

TARGETS

What is the norm for fair behaviour
When archaic values prejudice acceptance
To influence on ocean's current
Or know the meaning of the sun;
When all we know is all we judge
From cooling tide to comfort's warmth.
Why fan the frantic, leaping flame
Digesting deep progression's fuel,
What need fine plaudits to embrace
Aggression's fire of hidden ash.

Now the wriggling serpent rises
Uncomprising from its shroud,
Forks a vile ambiguous tongue,
Leaves a word's destructive wake
For ignorance to comprehend
Glibly passing on the flow
Practising neat the same mistakes,
And from his undenying coil
Unleashes sin's defiling lust
Into an earth drawn finale.

So now we turn neurotic eyes
On dusk's claustrophobic horizon,
Impression's mist rolls through hysteria's head
Eclipsing all in unsound logic
Where driven need replaces greed,
And passive yearning mellows sweet
When grand ideals invite neglect
Devalued through a maze of promise.
Reaction's spear thrown in spite
Contriving targets lost in decadence.

HARSH COMFORT

Word strong, emotion weak
Polishing dilemmas
Till they learn to speak,
Spread out the dumbness
Stretching harsh tremors
Feel comfort in numbness
Where nuance is lost
When matters are fading
And catches are tossed
To boundaries uncaring
With fielders degrading
The honour unsharing.
Controlled is the silence
When storm tongues are brewing,
Teeth-clenching violence
Subsides in retreat,
Forward the viewing
When left with defeat.
Lucid though pausing
Like comma-lilt verse
Effectively causing
Dull outdated prose
To praise with a curse
The thorn hidden rose.
Come forthright bold voice
Inhale dead passion,
Dull rhetoric's choice
In fever must burn
Exhale compassion
To comfort in turn.

13th May 1999

HOW SOON THE LIGHT

How soon the light reveals a sin
Where once my shadow fell.
Gone turmoil and torture's
Nerve-grinding retainers.
Recurring death's vision
Swirls a chilling haze
Across neurotic cells
Fills my spectre-throbbing skull
As drifting numbly
A waking nightmare dawns
To a mocking lark's reveille.
While a sun-fever's thick heat yawns
Gaping at my blistered being
Devoid of cunning and hostility.
No need for thought-conjuring,
Alone, as the world closes in,
My tenancy early expired
Regardless of unrequited time
And a ghost-waiting space
Where now a darkening veil falls
On a short gallow-beckoning morn.
These sounds are but the echoing past,
These eyes no purpose but to weep
Or see beyond the fear of fear
And dwell within a perfect sleep.

30th *June 1999*

TO SHIRLEY

The finest verse was never written,
The sweetest songs were never sung,
The greatest moments never lived,
The clearest bells were never rung.

The deepest spell was never broken
The bluest sky was never seen,
The perfect sun had never risen,
The best of times had never been.

The kindest heart was never broken,
The longest promise never kept,
The lover's vow was never fathomed,
The saddest eyes had never wept.

The faintest words were never whispered,
The loudest thunder never heard,
The calmest reason never uttered,
The fiercest storm had never stirred.

So it was until you came, my love,
This drinking from the never cup
An unslaked thirst no water quenched,
No future till my past filled up,
To dream in love's embracing sleep
Where fantasy is truth sublime,
Eternal in hope's perfect scheme,
Sweet vision in caressing rhyme.

6th March 2000

A WEAKENING STRENGTH

I see the coward fawn
His ego balloon deflated,
Care's famined psyche numbed
Sheltering a fist-filled violence
In a punch-bagged arrogance
Of self indiscipline.
Vanished the dapper persona
From an unkempt dawn's horizon
On surf-shone saddles
Of a dream-horse carousel
Riding a whirl pooled fairground,
Whipping unreined self-infliction
Down masochism's thorny trail
Like a dying orgasm
Dwindling on, in spite of full-spent loins.
Gone the strength to capitulate,
The nagging rhythm to destruction
Throbs, unphrased, in tuneless orientation;
He leaps in the pit's cacophony
Catches control's falling baton,
Waves a madness-thriving input
To a mocking tone-deaf world.

21st June 1999

DINING WITH THE GODS

Seek well the widening choice
Along free-fallen aspiration's path,
Turn up fresh volume on fever's ear
Perforating staid unbeaten drum
Away from non-distraction of comfort
In the eye-drooping, feet-up syndrome
Bequeathed by old saintly loafers.

Ambition's breath choking in haste
Stifles rationality's lung,
Skimps the mortar on the brick-filled day
Designing each weather shaken course
With a trembling heart's presumption,
Stirs a novice mix with expertise
Pointing trowel with novelty's panache.

Sip the entrée bowl of thick rich soup
Whilst presentation's main course hides
Beneath the garnish-glossed façade.
A studied menu's a la carte
From existence snack to living's feast
Holds no solution to stale hunger,
When contentment's diet fills no need.

28th April 1999

FORTY SHADES

Destroy my dark imaginings
Create my perfect dreams
Unveil unsung bravado
That perpetrates their schemes.

Climb care's slippery rainbow
Slide down hope's coloured joy,
Inhale the musk of influence
Adopted by each ploy.

Spill my ink of treason
Upon stark loyalist page,
Leave in doubt all justice
To another evil age.

Lift high the unstained chalice
That held King's poison sweet
When antidotes of fools' revenge
Was a compromised defeat.

Turn back derivation's clock
Where casual hands are rested
And see before the ants are spread
How clean the ground untested.

26th April 1999

WHERE GOES LOVE

When confidence has given all
What remains of thrusted valour
That knew not of each nerve's restraint
Whose prime shades mixed each colour
Upon blood's palette of design
To spread health's covering pallor.

Fair invitation felt no cause
To offer comfort or desire,
No hidden promise to detect
Love's mounting ash within the fire,
It is unseen, unheard, unfelt,
That only trust and dreams inspire.

Was slander's tale held in dispute
Unproven, yet could be believed
As though persuasion's tears had flowed,
Conjecture-filled, though ill-conceived
Defining fierce abhorrent ways,
Infatuation deep deceived.

When clouds of hate obscured fair skies
Tinged raw from heaven's afterglow,
There came a universe of light
Blinding sun and deafening snow,
Till all senses of existence
Set nature's chosen path aglow.

Adoration gloats on riches
Stolen from faith's generous heart
Tenderest of all the frailties
This chemistry that souls impart,
Overt and vulnerable as glass,
When drawn in strength, friendship departs.

10th March 1999

LATE MOVE

See objective cynicism
Focus through care's frail, subjective lens,
Plundering the treasure-sunken eye
On the moral high sea tempest
Where a calming slander sneers.
I sense overbearing sagas
Freeze on the unprotected ice,
For in the aged, cracking vision
Both old and young peer down too close
To see a melting fissure at their side.
They turn up the heat in the pulpit
Delivering an old text
To ears of no memory,
A glass fist lecturn-thumping
An awe- smashed congregation
With affordable ethics.
Spin time's vulnerable year
Through each season's orbit of disaster
Let genetic misfits toll their knell
Wash their suicidal plains with blood
Shrugging off the philosophic day
With an overwound clock of destruction.
So we fall in the target trap
Frantically aimed by updated stress,
Unaware of its late move.

18th February 1999

MISSING PIECE

Within sharp frameworks of design
A puzzled pattern forms
Interlocked through hell and heaven
Bored by stale perfection.
A shortfall on our bridge's span
Draws us gently to desire's high tide,
The whispering eddies flowing
To the facedown drowning pieces.

So to make those neat impressions
More aesthetic than our needs
As though true comfort was dependent
On balance of pedantic eyes
When all we could accumulate
Means less than aspiration's peak
From foothills of achievement
To the glacier of despair.

Now we seek the missing piece
That holds the text and symmetry
Of all in satisfaction's form
And give the world her rounded edge
To hear her axis humming sweet
And spin contentment's top,
Yet pause on havoc's daily run
And see the memory's puzzle clear.

27th January 1999

CARE

How lies compassion's script
Upon the rolling slope of sympathy
Distrusting of an unfelt push
Gaining patronised momentum
On the "not knowing how far to go"
Rely –poly, care running,
Fuss tailored, sincerely styled,
Syrup- laden syndrome.

So we heave on rusty brakes
Love's ratchet grinds concern,
Till groaning to a nervous halt
We analyse our frantic plan;
Why crank up misery's torque
From pressure turned to no avail
When dropping tools and standing back
Would ease the pain with feathered touch.

The interest paid on trouble
As multiplied through worry's gloom
So burst anxiety's bubble
By weaving care's creative loom.

5th March 1998

QUICK, QUICK, SLOW

When weakness in control concedes
In quiet debate to ponder,
A sweet retreat of unfelt wounds
And lets the mighty flounder,
For one spilt drop could multiply,
To whip the flood's tempestuous force
And turn a self-possessive eye
Upon an outward-bending course.

How floats vain, shallow victory,
No depth to drown uncoloured risk
Come, bathe in loser's sanctuary
Dwelling numb from ego's task.
Pierce presumption's bloated belly
Compulsion-crammed in gaseous hell,
Contaminate youth's virgin folly
And influence raw, static will.

So lives the strength of unsound timing
It matters less than nerve can say
That strips all reason from the rhyming
Leaving patience, weakness free.
What cause is there to draw the flame
Rising scant above the coals,
What need to fan inferno's game
Burning quick- fired unplayed roles.

14th January 1998

AVANT GARDE

There's nothing dates like avant garde
Splashed fresh by novelty's fountain
Dried swiftly in contentment's sun
Till dull hills become a mountain.

Sharp sayings stab the puerile air
With meaningless advantage gained
Yet used as wisdom's reference
To expedite sloth tongues untrained.

So our spotlight flickers briefly,
In naked symmetry we pose
Turning visual vanity
Into a tensified repose.

Comfortless, the driven challenge
Fills fresh bells with modern timbre
Till notes no longer peal new joy
When ropes are pulled in frantic clamber.

Chrysalis-shed vain flesh enthused
Life's fashion born devoid of style
Permanence in temporary state
No reason for a changing smile.

Ridiculed the previous set
As desperation waits the trends
Dictated by those clever fools
Who see the straight beyond the bends.

21st July 1999

THE MOVING WIRE

There's no such state as happiness,
Just varying degrees of cloud
That cast fate's lengthy shadow bare
Across a self-indulgent crowd.

No differential see we more
Than fortune disregarding health
When the former mocks the latter
And treads pride's moving wire with stealth.

Within our universal scope
We step towards the Milky Way
As much a change to race that light
Than tie those loose ends of our stay.

How long will we fill this craving
Bypassing all in vague pursuit
Where swift convenience fills the scales
To label gaining weight, 'astute.'

3rd August 1999

WASTE – BLINDNESS

WASTE	BLINDNESS
The	Happiness
Rich	And
Who	Misery
Cannot	Are
Spend	Put
Are	In
Poorer	True
Than	Perspective
The	By
Paupers	Sickness
Who	And
Can	Health

16th August 1999

SENTENCED TO JOY

Sentenced to joy for life
Reprieved in a blasé hell-hole
Optimism escaping
Through the bars of acceptance
Down solitary's drained wing
Of manic moon-facing cells.

I hear the dry eyed weepers
Sobbing vacuums of discontent
Where the norm of satisfaction
Drops in need's barometer
Till a sun surviving snow
Melts on dull, hardening ice.

Hail our fault praising ride
In thrill-revving momentum
Urging a falsified speed
Along the non-caring track
Grinding a sky-worth of gears
Within our system's synchromesh.

Now ends denial's term
The tear-waves cease to flow
A season's act begins
And we know not where to go
Our vehicle lies stranded
Where the winds of freedom blow.

28th September 1999

THE LEARNING

Look back down Triassic way
The crudest of all beauty
Strutted and roamed at leisure
Fed upon weaker species
Gaining territory for spite
Characterless in survival,
Existential destruction
Numbed with gluttony's lust
In carnivorous or herbal gut,
No progress of pleasure
In the stillness of time
Wallowing in predatory bliss
Down the pecking order of existence.
Waking to success of well being
Hunting batteries fully charged
Death's urgent ritual begins
The generation chase ascends
Leaving the burden of conscience
To a quiet extinction,
Slowly a civilised blind descends
We peer through micro chinks
At man's involved performance
And clear as our comprehension
Of universal nothingness
His earthly input remains unchanged.

5th *January 1999*

A THORN DEFILED

A thorn defiled
Festers in denial
Retracts a hidden point
Tasting the undrawn blood
From a wounded vision.
Comes night's throbbing hour,
An orgasm of spite
Plumbs the bowels of retribution
Twisting the gut of justice
Beyond placid well-being.
A dormant reflex springs
Convulsed in hate's momentum
In an ordeal of delight.
Nerve ends numbed in silence
Muffle a living sound box
Held by death's dark receiver
Where the uninviting ear
Burst's revenge's inner canal
Savouring delirium's flood
Turning back the heart's clock
To a rape-filled savage beat,
Like a thorn defiled.

20th October 1999

A DUBIOUS TREASURE

Flexing of fresh muscled neurons
Where stale, insipid plains are worn,
Tread deep footholds of dejection
When unprepared a smile is torn.
With words engraved the wise have fled
From tombs that cover noble deeds
Not for them the praise in passing
That occupies their spacious needs.

When loose-eyed monsters ogle wild
Unspent libido's sacrifice
Fine dignity is overwhelmed
And loads lost luck on unthrown dice.
For were the taming of desire
A natural calming measure
Then we would never need this life
That seeks a dubious treasure.

Guile's trajectory clears the earth
Leads a devious way for men
Returns to inhibition's cave
A trembling lion in his den.
Courage bled on soaked up passion
Flag colours run on twilight's field,
Worthless and noble side by side
Berserk, the callous axes yield.

3rd November 1999

A DEATH BEFORE DYING

Butchered! A breed on a Bosnian field
Anarchy dawns, blood shadow's vile passion,
Ethnic divisions drawn up to be killed
In a carnage gripping season's fashion.
Babies on bayonets pinned to the sky,
Mothers too numb to feel the mass raping,
Depravity's stench stays, never to lie
Locked in a psyche, never escaping.
Inherent was the blinding Muslim strain
Cross-bred through the troubled Balkan craving
That Tito calmed with communism's stain
Leaving oppression's legacy raving
Yearning to shed a tear before crying
Drowning the pain, a death before dying.

29th November 1999

RUMBA NIGHTS

I see a pier whose smiling lights inspire
A land of pleasing values in a dance
Where ingrained lifelong tempos never tire
Along old Cuban shores with souls entranced.
A gentle urgency with rapture blends
Melting an ice wall 'round a nervous eye
Where cramped desire her inhibition ends
As bongos patter to the naked sky

Untamed, she drifts across moon- dripping sand
A body drawn in supple -hipped design
Melodious passion oozes through her hands
Intoxicating love on rhythm's wine.

How smooth the spell reality invites,
Star floating on those distant Rumba nights.

8th December 1999

UNQUIET THOUGHTS

The finest poetry is never written
It lingers deep in archives of the mind
Like an orchard with its fruit unbitten
Remaining there unseen before the blind.
Words are but the vehicle for meaning
So often read and lost in obscured haste
When convinced no knowledge there for gleaning
It matters not the motive nor the taste.

Like verse do we conceal devotion
Our deepest love is never truly felt
Hidden deep in labyrinths of emotion
Awaiting for the icebound heart to melt.
Let not the sleep of apathy be still
Make unquiet thoughts erupt against their will.

19th May 1999

NOVELTY'S DISCIPLINE

Entranced by contemporary vision
Sweet as infant breath upon the first snow
A returning sun's disappointing glow
Spreads a Spring-weaved pattern's indecision,
And all is lost in dignity's fine shroud
That hides desire's incipient unheld breath
Borrowing for one moment unfelt death
Nourished on flair's pasture so fickly ploughed.

Novelty's discipline obeyed yet brief
Blind stamped drilling on compulsion's order
Where a Kingdom's rebel will is banished
By acting wonderment's fantasy thief
Who plundering boredom's narrow border
Pauses not till time's sweet spell is vanished.

11th February 1999

FARMER FOP AND URCHIN

A farmer draws on his pipe
Blows a thin veil at the sunset
Treads on a pale young lettuce
Stirring up a fight
With survival's recoil.
On the apex of breeding
Chinless waffle's erosion
Unreels a class-grained line,
It falls, yet never losing pace
Fades in sickly gesture.

Back in the urban zoo
An urchin squats on the kerb
Drinking last week's crust
In yesterday's puddle
Cheeks bloating, cherry fresh with health.
Marauding clouds, rain clad,
Spill across the frowning sun
As farmer, fop and urchin
Draw upon a living urge
Frantic, yet becalmed as one.

20th *June 1996*

LET US CONTINUE TO LIE

Let us continue to lie
Filling diplomacy's bag
With as much democratic energy
As absolute truth allows,
Buffing the jaded sparkle
Of smug intellect dull-bred.

Our engine turns and roars,
Pistons awake from their thick sleep
Hot oil drips and sizzles
In a fluid friction's rise and fall,
A bonnet points the cross-road,
The smell of living begins.

And as we drive, regardless
Of fury, faith and circumstance,
Love embroiders our design,
Faceless strangers' shadows form,
We turn just sideways on and blink
To glimpse convenience of the facts.

28th *June 1995*

SURREALIST DAY

Visions and shadows swirling
Through yesterday's future
As we pass waiting nothingness
Giving off futile essence
From our stark being
Criticising empty materialism
Yet existing in an ancient shell
Housing past and future generations
With jealous walls and nervous roofs
And a secret garden's hanging tree.

How blows my draconian day
With a worldly snort of disgust,
Town and country wisdom merging
Down escapist insular funnel
Focusing on a floating island's freedom
Where fish deny the spear and net
And I rejoice in doubt-filled shade
Shackled by contentment
Drink life from an insidious barrel
Rolling it to the unreturning tide
Endeavouring to replace with goodness
From boredom's futile shore.

7th June 1995

CYCLING

High on contemplation's saddle
Inspiration sprung,
See the waiting track
Whispering from a tarmac silence,
'Away, away, this is the day',
On fearless pedals
Hurricane geared,
An accumulation of spirit form
Hear the singing spokes
On momentum's orbit
A gasping lyric run
Coasting and spurting for position.
A burnt tyres pungency
Grips the frantic air
A crowd screams for an outside chance
Yet trusting to finish
In victory or defeat,
Free-wheeling the last lap.

13th July 1995

OLD IDEALS

Tell me, my friend, do you care,
Really care, when offspring stray
From your over protective fold,
Do you know of love, that she
In truth, should give nothing in return
For all you have bestowed,
Nothing more than duty will demand
From their conception till your death.

No; pride has led your willing hand
To a Victorian time-warped corner
Where you expect unearned respect,
Paranoia has you by the throat
Grips and clings convincingly
Like an unforgiving octopus
Just below the surface,
You breathe the light that cannot calm the lung.

Were you the child for which your parents yearned,
Did you know rejection and dismay
We have all been there, back and in between,
They stepped too close and lost their sight
Yet still the old ideals are handed down
Like the haunting of a dull refrain;
We see our beneficiaries weep,
We know but do we really care.

2nd May 1995

BETWEEN PROGRAMMES

Finger flitting fever,
Across keys of technology,
A programmed face defies
My idiot brain;
One dimensional bliss
A kind of peace slumbering,
Returning with a fresh blankness
To encompass a lesser meaning
From a darkness ever increasing
In bewildering format
Widening a superior gap
Between that which I will never see.
Could you not pause for air
In your robotic brilliance
And breathe not so much the how
That causes man and worlds to change,
The philosophies and sentiments,
Present and future values -
No not the how, but why!

25th April 1995

TRICKS

Magic an influence,
Illusion spreading
Power of emotion
In an uncut cake
Of hidden fruits,
Smooth as uncracked icing.
Alabaster countenanced
Expressionless as death
Our world's demise
Ignorant of its condition
Turns an ungreased axis
Gradual through current experiences
Sudden on retrospect
Dwelling a pragmatic hour
Till complacency's erosion
Crumbles with tricks of ruin,
All explanation meaningless
Through ploy, sleight of dexterity,
Private intellectuals
Becoming public fools;
For possessed with all knowledge
Repeated mistakes await.

6th *November 1995*

Ivor Vernon Smith

WE THE BRITISH

As a nation, we the British
Have learnt better than any other
How to tolerate and crawl,
Form orderly queues without complaint
Be reserved and modest to a fault
Somehow merging success with failure
Stiffen our upper lips with resolve;
Evaporating like Summer snow
When set-backs form and troubles loom
Quietly winning against all odds.

As a nation, we the British
Instinctively discriminate
Friend from foe, chains from freedom,
Living as one in a warring peace.
One day posterity will judge
How we the British survived
When having fought the world and won,
Draining Commonwealth and Empire dry,
With no-one left to beat or fool
We turned upon ourselves and lost!

December 1994

RIDERS

The
world
is
a
merry-go-round
accelerating
out
of
control
finally
flinging
its
riders
to
oblivion

Somehow
we
must
develop
a
method
to
slow
it
down
regardless
of
time
and
cost

Not
only
must
we
find
who
first
threw
the
switch
but
comprehend
his
dubious
philosophy

1st October 1996

THE DARK SHORE

In the haven of a dream
The night sea beckons
And I like gentle flotsam
Am with tidal magnet drawn
Upon the rollers of my lust,
The shadow forms and fades,
Crying in fear-drowned logic
I change the stroke, but no,
There is no variation on this
A frantic, deadly theme.
The murmuring shingle,
Bass to the seagull's falsetto,
Drifts yet stays, appears and fades,
Clings, relaxed, soaked in rhythm,
Breathing night with moon's caress,
Then with a knave's deceit
Twists the unassuming tide
On an undetected ebb,
And I with fresh, determined strokes
Swim within my circle of desire
In an all-consuming light
Till the blackness of the blind descends
Leaving me alone and pallid
Riding reality's nightmare
Out upon the dark shore.

10th February 1995

Ivor Vernon Smith

MR. BIG

Strained the rules on deep integrity
In this game where knaves are trumps
For a service that denies gratuity
So makes the ride avoid the ramps,
Points a path toward fortuity
Yet on the weak with fervour stamps.

Self-delusion's lost resistance
So tragic with a mind split keen,
Just like a mirror, at a distance
A poor reflection's 'might have been',
Yielding blind to greed's persistence,
A dying character's stealing scene.

See the power-spun web is weaving
The avaricious spider grins
With a gullible world believing
In his dark mesmeric sins
With the world and self deceiving
As lust's amoral trek begins.

The ragged man need not impress
With wit or fine honed intellect,
Weakening strength cannot redress
This balance which the mind selects,
Those pedals that the feet depress
Are all corruption's drive selects.

8th February 1996

JUDGE AND JURY

The inward journey
Winds wearily down introversion's path
Fading before the eclipse of freedom,
A shadowing motherless earth
Bearing ill love to a silent infatuation
Scoring a perfect own goal
In misery's losing game.
Repression's muted hammer
Drives deep the passive nail
Through self-indulgent layers
Of fears unresisting fabric,
A guilt-weighed secret
Spilt before the psyche's jury
Swayed by hell's biased judge,
Grimed deep through the devil's prosecution
Cleansed raw by purgatory's defence,
Emotion's trauma holding court
Frowns as hysteria sums up,
A life-sentence pronounced
On plaintiff and defendant.

9th February 1995

BEAT THE RETREAT

Swift in retreat we re-adjust,
Swift as a swallow's wind-crossed flight
Subtle and fine betraying trust
Those reassuring arms invite.
Straight excuse or crooked reason
Are spread before the fact of doubt
Concealed beyond a hint of treason
With words of love from heart devout.

How gentle confidence does yield
Along the dark insidious way
Till weeping on the harvest field
It now succumbs in sun-killed hay.
Yet there are some designing schemes
That glide and spin like meadowlarks
Whilst no-one solves those devious dreams
And famine seeks the weak and poorest
Till only herding blinds and needs.
So hold this numbed erroneous play
Lose the dice down fortune's gutter
And in retreat gain victory's day
By forming fresh from losing's stutter.

12th January 1996

LOST LOVE

What remains
When the final words
Are shaken out,
What enflames
When deep passions gel
The hollow shout.

Charmless wit
Articulate flood
Drowned on the lips,
Point-made spit
Aimed at the quiet eye
Tearful it slips.

Bored decay
Festering and wilting
Wallows in hate,
Wartime at play
Ties a fine noose
Silencing mate.

24th April 1995

THE SCHEME OF THINGS

You reached aloft and clutched the perch
That sagged beneath the untold s train
Enburdenment destined to snap stout chains
Yet holding beyond the will of hope,
Rekindling a subterranean fire.

You wondered how you blossomed forth
When needs were scattered on arid land
Knowing no former yield, an entombed
mole scratching for freedom
Beneath the cracked dissipated face that never
knew a smile in these torrid climes,
Tortured within by countless decades of impotency
Reaping a harvest of senility everlasting.

But still you came with faltering step
Limp as a willow from the storm
Senses reeling from the fray
Fresh clean air purifying stale pores
Inhaling a wind-swept land.
Weaned from sweat of doubting philosophies,
Strangling this virgin mind with frozen logic
On circumlocutions endless roundabout.

And so softened static arteries
Dormant veins now to flow unceasingly
Their unswerving course channelled
Through prejudice and unfelt causes
Built from flints of fear
Tearing at the soft flesh of the inner self
Cocooned in a mortar of smugness
Till you groped for air as the lungs choked.

And you filtered into the scheme of things

Not knowing how, nor caring why,
But still you prayed
Begging forgiveness for you knew not what,
Till drinking unspoilt rain that fell
On remaining parched fissures
You opened weary wondrous eyes
Gazing forever upon a living world.

FACADE

Hot breath that clung,
Poised languidly on icy air
Unthawed by a reluctant sun
On a day hushed to the tree-tops
By the soundless fall
Of this white silence
Blanketing the earth's passive face,
Frozen rigidity yet prevailing
On a sea of crushed waves,
Descending with forced calm
On a turbulent brow,
Virginal frigidity yet denying
Lust of a torrid mind,
Snow weighing heavily open boughs
That once bore Summer leaves
With egotistical pride,
Foliage grasping greedily
At shafts of sunlight
Peering through impenetrable depths,
Till complacent greenery trembled
Beneath the breath of the first Autumn chill,
Retreating deeper in the forest,
Tired legs no longer answering
The intolerant brain's call,
To lay panting in the ferns
Waiting for the tireless hunter.

1974

HERITAGE OF DUST

Where did they go?
Young men of the earth,
Planting their hearts,
With the muscle of youth
They sought not for glory
They sought not for truth
But with power in their eyes,
Sought the rich fruit,
Secured by the land's bank,
Withdrawn at high interest
From its fertile vault,
Built before time;
The black crust
Cooled by a sea of sweat,
Cursed by broken backs,
Repeating forefathers' oaths.

This heritage of dust
Staining lungs and pores
As scarred hands grope
For freedom from his dungeon,
Then tired eyes blink
At the white sky's welcome;

Where did they go,
Young men of the earth,
Was their valley so barren,
Did they not know its worth?

November 1973

Ivor Vernon Smith

THE LAST BOMB

Blood spat, dark
Grey vein's eruption;
Fallen, the word vomit
Oozing down blistering cheeks
From a promise - throbbing tongue.

Body splinters stuck
In the voodoo sky,
Sun's angered flush
Moon's sighing hush,
Star's dreaming light.

Ice venom seeded
Festering fields, flowering
Amid the poppy wasters,
Memory torn ragged,
Love's last kiss frozen.

Scarlet waves rushing
Through a mind's naked haze,
Corrupt and fair victims
Blend as to nothing
Death's tomb-shaping dust.

A monotone swansong
Fills the unbreathing mist,
Lost is the nameless space,
Lost in the ghost-levelled ground -
Equal now beyond all choice.

**ptar*1984*

MIRROR, MIRROR.......

You itch with vanity's passion
Tearing at the scab of fashion,
Layering lipstick's classy pout
Till coarse the untrained words drop out.

Who really cares just how you do
Mascara, be it black or blue,
Or dagger nails in green or pink,
Or how your dress falls as you slink.

Or whether shoes be wedged or flat,
Or why things should be this or that;
Does anybody really care?
If you or your scent hang in the air.

Who are you, with new nose and ears
Disguising those self-conscious fears;
A damned good wash is all you need
To form true bloom from nature's seed.

Keep your clothes when styles are changing,
Time her wardrobe's re-arranging;
Why succumb to the mode's confusion,
'Tis merely novelty's illusion.

26th October 1979

HELL'S GATHERING STORM

Excitation bent upon the blackening collarbone
Burnt as the books of turmoil in a
frightened age,
A dictator swelling in seconds
Within the startled walls
Of a passive vagina succumbing to
the rising ecstasy
In blind submission, borne on wings
of disciplined hysteria.

This urgency of puppet-whipping
so often denied
The jack-booted indolence of sullen sheep
Straying from far flung boundaries,
Nomads of destruction belching with
the swill of propaganda
Vomiting with one accord upon the
passive Star of David.

A strutting demi-god Satan-powered
on Europe's threshold,
Playing treaty gambits
with endless pawns,
Democracy a spineless word, misspelt
by diplomacy's gullible pen
Dipped deep in sincerity's invisible ink
On the grime-shredded parchment
headed "Trust".

Cymbal-clashing, a goose-stepping
arrogance was nurtured
In early adolescence, products of teutonic breeding
Swelling 'neath the overture's rising
crescendo in mighty voice

Resounding, fists air-punching
with group-minded extraversion
Soul-tingling down the lane of a thousand
scarlet banners.

Bedeviled destiny's plot, to violate
unsuspecting humanity
Biting deep the sinew, destroying light
with vigour unrepentant
Gripping the hang-nail of apathy in a
fearshone whitlow
Lanced under an anaesthetic of numbed
disbelief,
Yet believe they did, helpless from the
eyeless needle of persuasion.

Suffering innocence, forever the conscience of mankind,
Till then; a spurious gesture to flit
across that sadistic brow,
Breathing hope upon minds,
seeking touch upon the thread of compassion
And so the starless night was born,
Conceived by an ageless lust,
A burning womb, sterile in the memory's
afterglow.

15th May 1975

Ivor Vernon Smith

FREUD

He called himself a Godless Jew,
Yet was it really strictly true,
Though not indeed a pious man
Who else to bear the burden than
He who drew each hidden thorn
From shrouded minds with thoughts unborn.

To him each dream another star
Lighting the night with hope afar
Flickering with promise along the way
When contempt and apathy had their say,
Deaf ears, blind eyes, all satisfied
That evil words must be defied.

Often abused and misunderstood
Jeered and scorned by men of wood,
Protesting too much with fists of guilt
As pride and prejudice was spilt,
Murmuring dissent when back was turned,
Contradicting, but how they learned.
Darkening clouds of depressions deep
Unmoving in repression's sleep,
Unseen the hidden sun on high
Beyond the still Vienna sky.
Till winds of change they blew, they blew,
First shafts of light, he knew, he knew!

The id a child to play its games,
Amid the wild impassioned flames,
Till super ego dominated
This urge it so abominated;
Now Oedipus recall the deed
That made forgetting such a need.

Whispers form a couch he heard
When sex was still a dirty word,
To will that hidden stones be cast
Revealing traumas of the past,
To run through the psyche's corridors
Opening all the bolted doors.

He taught the memory how to think,
Grasping wrists on sanity's brink,
The world declined his outstretched hand
When once they did not understand,
Till cameras clicked and eyes shone wide,
Developing negatives lost inside.

Between the symptoms and the cause
There might elapse a lifetime's pause,
Not just this studied sublimation
Earned universal reputation,
Oh no! Immortality his role,
Bequeathing to mankind his soul.

1974

THE QUIET PLACE
A Marriage Sonnet

May each aspiration and ambition
With fine dreams forever bear fruition
As together you walk life's tangled maze
Of cul-de-sacs and lost deceptive way,
Until you come upon the quiet place
Where true perspective shows her perfect face
Judging not the conversational flow
But more when silence tends to grow
To shun incipient flame's illusioned leap
Re-kindling afterglow's devotion deep,
Yet if love were all, you would never need
The Gods to smile or fate to ever heed
So even on hell's raw and blackest night
A distant star of hope glows constant bright.

15th November 1992

DRY INHIBITION

It's a funny thing this drinking
When all the bullshit waffles out,
No-one seems to care who's thinking
Or what the hell its all about.

They stand like men and drink all night
With swollen gut and beetroot cheek,
As songs which seem to them alright
Swell forth whilst others dare to speak.

With soppy eyes blurred pink with smoke
They lurch and sway around the place.
And with their grimy fingers poke
The chests of cornered fools they chase.

Those raucous parties they attend
Extravert logic to impart,
And should one fail to comprehend
They think you've neither wit nor heart.

Man rides cloud dreams escaping fate
And shifts his image with the tide,
Some drown in alcoholic state
To lubricate truth's rougher side.

Yet wipe away all interference
The shouting, vomit and the sweat,
Deep beneath the incoherence
Is closest to the truth you'll get.

8th February 1984

LISTENING

See the sun is rising
Do not shout today,
She whispered with her eyes,
Yesterday was winter
Stars hung in their still heavens
And a tired old moon
Yawned in his eclipse
There was mercy squandered
By the nightfall
On each tempting wind blowing
Across the silent earth
Voices absorbed within the snow
Lay aground in muted sighs
And naught but a tingling ear
Remained of the loud day
In the listening of the pensive trees.

9th February 1976

THERE WAS A TIME

There was a time
Many voices ago
When silence hung
In dark festoons
From a tree-top congregation
And the forest hymn
Was sung to the breathing of the wind
With the grey leaves
Turning upon each crumbling paradox
A rustling accompaniment
In the moonlit nave
Where once the sun had blushed
In her maternal pride
Until the shame of man.

16th March 1976

BRIGHTON SHADES

Regency Squares and Georgian Lanes
Old Steine, Pavilion and the Dome,
It's trips and dips and hazy ships
And a beach that some call home.
A band plays Dixie by the pier
A tall white skyline stuck in the sun,
It's rides and slides and crashing tides,
And the old Volk's Railway run.

The Smiths and Jones are booking in
The week-end cliche's never fade,
It's rude and lewd and a beach that's nude
For the dirty mac brigade.

There's banana skins by litter bins,
Adorning crust-filled sandwich bags,
It's fun and sun on the Martha Gunn
As the scorching noon-day drags.

There's white-legged girls of early Summer
With 'kiss me quick' by a moon-filled sea,
It's dances, romances and lost golden chances,
And there's candy-floss for tea.

It's the Windmill scene of Rottingdean
And the broken pier of yesteryear,
Cars and bars with lights like stars
And there's cockles in your beer.

The pungent pubs and junkie clubs,
Lend decadence her form,
Where in the dark, a broken heart,
Hides deep from the glittering norm.

Below the proms, the clattering toms,
Deceive the watchful law,
Lost brats and prats in silly hats,
And what the Butler saw.

The hanky-panky moon grins down
On the white bum-bobbing shore,
With each mincing gay upon display
And a sailor's shrieking whore.

For all its overt shallowness,
A heart still drives this breathless town,
That meets and greets on salt-aired streets,
This ruby in the Sussex crown.

1992

VAN GOGH

What manifests itself on canvas plain
Through fingers itching with art's neurosis
Revealing genius latent since birth
Of a mind's landscape trembling for the freedom
So denied by the progress of man
On a sightless planet of indifference.

Now the banner-free hand exposed,
Moving noiselessly across the new born countryside
Challenging each unseeded patch to bloom evergreen,
Capturing an unrepeated moment
On time's gladdening face,
Bequeathing a thought for posterity.

How drifted the Dutchman's mind?
Standing chest-high in golden grain,
Clutching brush with numbed hand,
Stirring palette with an unrecognized fever
Dark ingredients of the baying wind
And the lull when August warmth caressed him.

Fierce strokes that flourished on a clear noon,
Each thrust reflecting co-ordination,
Unequalled by any other touch and sight,
A soul at peace with the scene,
At war with its own repressions,
Gulping greedily on the land's breath.

He knew God this man,
Not for many a year by clasped hand
But with unbending knees held firm
And lost eyes gazed unblinking
Up a mocking road to a self-made Calvary
Bearing his easel for humanity.

November 1973

SIEGE

Now sweet reproach of innocence
Turn me the cold eye of your truth,
My cross it swiftly burns and I
Know little of your perfect youth.

I never knew one perfect day
When anguish deep in natural form
Would dare escape those treasured dreams
And let me from this vortex swarm.

Rattled loud the memory's chain,
Pinned upon the torturer's wall,
The symmetry which once was mine
Is there dispersed beyond recall.

The secrets now have built their web
Love's tower has toppled in their wake,
One can but lay the siege to ruins -
No more a citadel to take.

11th March 1983

CHILD OF MAY

Gentle form pass through the softening air,
Caressing all with unspoilt beauty gold-spun hair
Cascading flow on carefree shoulders,
nature groomed
Unstudied in her perfect space, she
filled with joy perfumed
In garden patch to tread those infant ways,
For pleasured memories of those glowing days
And to the sun, rolled in her sparkling wake
It seemed sheer purpose for fates course to take
A long embrace to kiss the purest brow
Which yielded but sweet innocence,
As did the spring-time bough.

The doting eyes that held reflected love
Remained a camera for the sheltered dove,
For in her iridescence, a negative lay blown
In many treasured shades of bliss
her life had ever shown,
Too soon the warbler of the night
would cast a starlit spell
And set the unfelt genesis a worldly
dream to dwell
Within the maiden sleeper, to pluck
her first full rose
And watch each trembling petal, fall
from its languid pose.

My pen has quivered through the night
With ponderous thoughts that meet her sight,
Will she, this blessing born to me,
Observe the love conceived through Thee,
As I transfixed before her gaze,
Tremble, as she walks life's maze.

Ivor Vernon Smith

1971

THE TIGHT-ROPE WALKER

The high-wire sags beneath his weight
As looking down he spies his fate,
All sewn up in a sawdust ring,
So why not have a final fling.

Deportment fine with eloquent poise,
Perfecting all his many ploys,
He treads life's tight-rope with a sneer,
Not for him a stolen tear.

His creditors watch with baited breath,
As he trips on gaily to the death,
Juggling and hopping a merry dance,
Pulling strings on the outside chance.

Now he makes his final bow,
With panache as only he knows how,
He waves and then his grip releases,
And bankers swoop to pick the pieces.

November 1973

FAREWELL

What do you see in the fire, old man?
Is that the flame of your life?
Soon it will fade into ash old man,
That flame filled with sorrow and strife.

Nobody with you tonight, old man,
No-one to tell you your worth,
See how the smoke fills your eyes old man,
As it did on the day of your birth.

Can you recall one moment in time
When the world stood still and you knew
That you felt the pulse of the Universe
And all heaven and hell passed through.

When did the sun start to set, old man?
Turning your day into night,
Unable to stifle a lifetimes tears,
When even the moon lost her light.

What did you do with your life, old man?
Have you one dream to remember?
Or has your star dimmed forever tonight,
As you gaze at the last glowing ember.

November 1973

I WANT TO BE A COMPUTER DAD

I want to be a computer, Dad,
And side-step the morrow you planned,
To grow within this century's bud
And flower in that silicone land.

Look old man, wipe the dust from your eye,
The time that you passed was not mine,
The stars alone will remain on high
when the micros perpetually shine

Take up the slack on your reasoning
To watch the ripe universe skinned
Where death will be merely cold seasoning
And you sigh to the ends of the wind;

Where man will be born into leisure
As he leaps to the stars at his will,
Where joy is an art less the pleasure
With sleep-programmed minds never still.

Gone then the freedom to procreate
As the videos record each move
Of those with IQ's below the rate
Till they fill the conditioning grove,

When you awake to a time and place
With the hour of disease long denied
And gaze deep into my digital face
Will you see where the tear-wells are dried?

1979

THE DARK SHEET

I slid beneath the dark sheet
That caressed your silken body
And eased the turbulence
Of my burdened heart
Into your waiting warmth
Lying there locked
In pleasure's bosom
Feeling the sighing stars
Gently pressing their tender clouds
Slowly, slowly ever slipping
Back the dark sheet
On a reluctant, naked dawn.

4th February 1982

WATERLOO BRIDGE

Hovering between life and death
The smell of meths upon his breath,
Lying shivering in that hole
Having drunk away his soul,
Caring naught for man nor reason
Longing for next summer season,
When he would beachcomb 'long the Thames
And pick some drab discarded gems,
So he could boast and he could hum
What man of substance he'd become
To store them like a frantic spider
Till tempted by a swig of cider.

The sallow, lean, unshaven face
And stumbling legs that knew no grace
Formed an ill connected shape
To grope down streets of no escape
In boots string-laced to beg and roam,
Then stealing to his archway home,
To shut out the world with a newspaper sheet
And count the eager homeward feet,
His protests unheard from that pavement bed
At those rumbling neighbours overhead,
Stale cigarette butt in his lips
Then to a troubled dreamworld slips.

18th February 1975

CATS!

Persistent pleasure principle prevails,
Lethargic, lithesome, lick loving living,
Feline freedom frolicking fearlessly,
Springing spritely, sure-footed sparrow-ward,
Branch balancing beauty, breath baiting birds,
Tigerish tenacity tantalised,
Mouse mauling murderers meditating
Sun-soaking schemers, sly, sleek, scratching spivs,
Lap-laying lovingly, luck-filled leisure,
Purring prowlers, playful panthers preening
Full feather-silk fur, fresh from fish-feasting,
Self-centred survivors sleepily stretching,
Noiselessly nonchalant napping nestlers,
Calculating comforters, callous.....
CATS!

A MEMORY'S BONDAGE

Let us not speak of times past
Or things that might have been
Nor how you make each memory last
I know not what you mean.

How you prayed the war would end
When on your bedroom floor you knelt,
How could I really comprehend
I know not what you felt.

You recall when first you held
Your first born to the air,
And though you blink where tears have welled,
I know not why you care.

You speak of nights where sorrow
Has cast her endless sigh
Upon the red-eyed morrow,
I know not why you cry.

You begin a mild confession
Of some impetuous scheme,
To end in wild transgression,
I know not why you dream.

You remember Summers hot and long
Those halcyon days so missed
When love embraced till Autumn song,
I know not who you kissed.

You say there is little virtue
In these times so insincere
And yet did not your past desert you,
I know not why you fear.

Ivor Vernon Smith

NONSENSE

We need the nonsense in our lives,
The safety valve when all else fails
When tidal waves of stress arrive
As hope beyond horizon sails.

How fine the measuring of souls
By perfect hands where good is right
When channelled to the drive goals
A pleasured madness fills each sight.

They once imposed a Godly will
And brought their manacles of love,
Yet never knew the laughing skill
To point the novice heart above.

When lightning forked and deeds were fouled
Word storms had quenched Athenian skies,
And Rome's corruption cried aloud -
O for a farce to lift thine eyes!

On daily wings we skim the earth
And race one breath from sanity,
This crowded sphere holds hidden mirth
And stifles tight humanity.

See how frustration's naked son
With broken spears and undrawn knives
Who knows not if to die or run;
We need the nonsense in our lives!

Ivor Vernon Smith

A 1970'S APPETITE

Molars cracking, molars splitting
Lips a'smacking, tongues a'flitting
Ever closer to the marrow
Picking like a famished sparrow,
The naked bone saliva shone
When all last clinging meat had gone,
Would that one could savour
An insatiable palate, this flavour
For eternity's taste to wallow
In the inevitable swallow
Incensing taste buds so provoked
By that which avarice had soaked,
And with this saturation done,
To compete within temptation's run.

Molars cracking molars splitting
Naught remaining worth the spitting,
Chew the slivers one by one
The self-made famine has begun,
And now the once too tolerant creditors
Have been replaced by drooling predators,
Whose belch-filled bellies and gluttonous minds
In focused eyes which avarice blinds,
Have picked the lean and fat and gristle
Then lain grease-skinned in sands to sizzle
Whilst yearning for more fatted prey,
And lying there burnt black with greed
When all those wants become a need
Tongues finger-licking ere next killing,
With toothpicks prodding beefy filling.

A CANTERBURY DREAM

Concave, the conscience tied,
The dais raised by men denied
The bread, the wine of bawdy days
When few belched hard in sacrifice;
Down musty crypt where gargoyles lurk
Amidst the organ tremors
Normanic spirits clank dusk's chain
Clasped to the ritual bosom-work
Of the essence of man and.....and....
And I! Chaucer led,
Trusting to the greed of men
Bequeathed my upturned chalice
To the scarlet altar, flushed in fever,
Drowning in the watered cross
Of minds sweated to the scaling crust,
Revering the liquid image, endured
To capacity, in the silver thread of promise
Lingering in the ghost-light year
Of non-existent time.

And yet, beneath the flagstone, dogma-laid,
Treasures which no agnostic mind dare prize,
Remain thorn pinned in the briar's creed
Preached before the Word
Had turned the throbbing ear
Earthward, pole-dividing in purpose,
And providing all belief
In the internal enigma.

Sun resistant in the cooling weed
Slaking a profound thirst, an internal spring,
Eternally sprung in....in.....
In the cloistered echo of harsh knights
Plunging steel, glinting in profanity

On the sacrificial steps,
The futile cry, hung plaintive on distant vespers,
A king, a bishop mutual in undecided love.
And we, the passed pawns of circumstance,
Await the theologians late move,
Raise our voices to Gothic spires,
Hang on the sky's note
And watch the pilgrims flock the fields,
And watch.....and watch....and wait.

7th July 1975

PRIDE

Polish hard the mirror,
This mirror you have cherished,
Reflecting heritage so dear
To the heart's lust
And the eye's passion;
You felt this force
When first conceived
On that restless night
As the careless wind howled,
Fighting the first breath
With tears of pride;
Many a battle won
Since that far off morn,
Many a licked wound
Through malicious thorn,
The agony wells
Within the inner self,
Lips are bitten
Tear-stained cheeks are turned
Clenched, white fists restrained,
Only the soul's mirror
Reveals the hair-line crack.

November 1973

ANOREXIA NERVOSA

Bone-shaping
Phobia's eyes dwell
On a fat mirror's frown

Falls weeping
From the lying scales,
A feather, fashion-flown.

Mind -raping;
Yielding to a dark will
A deadly fast has grown.

Blind leaping
Where time's pool grows stale
In weightless dreams to drown.

Yet hoping
A famined land lies still
Trembling at the dawn.

Or sleeping,
To dream of flesh until
Awakening forlorn.

10th June 1987

OUR ALEX

In deep mid-winter you were born
When apprehension froze the ground,
How soon your presence warmed my heart
To melt the snow skies all around.
Then in your eyes a comfort grew,
You were my counsel there to be
My strength when falling, till I saw
My Alex gazing up at me.

Stand firm and straight, be clear and true
Your tiny hand will lead me on,
I see the man behind the child
Though that dear face is never gone.
The world of wealth where men indulge
Would not exist for me to see,
Gain, power or gold could not compare
With Alex gazing up at me.

To see you grow and play with zest
Is pleasure more than love can say
And though a tantrum makes a fight
Your character just builds this way.
Dusk born, your star it flickers bright,
No sweeter nights could ever be
With gentle head about to rest,
Than Alex gazing up at me.

When I am wearying of life
And wonder what I did was right
There comes a feeling through the mist
That shows with joy this hidden light,
To kiss once more my darling son
And know that there will never be
No sight more precious than this one

Of Alex smiling up at me

2003

PART II – Sonnets

PAUPER KING

A pauper with no right to ever be,
Paranoid grasp on intangible wealth,
Obsessive spider weaves with frantic glee
Blind to necessities, leisure and health.
Intense the drama in sheer quantity
Building a Midas syndrome, self enslaved,
Existing devoid of all quality
To seek security beyond the grave,
Counting balance on abstract interest
Of calculated meanness doomed to fail,
Leaves ridicule breathing thoughts unimpressed
Regretting untouched pleasures unfurled sail.
What price this thrift and self denial pays
For all the wasted wisdom of your days.

13th June 1996

DREGS

Bouquet leaking
Across dying air,
Dank cellar creaking
With pleasure's wine,
An untrodden grape
I dreamt was mine.

Sediment shaken
Clouds my reverie,
Love is broken
Slowly to fall,
No bitter sip
I drink it all.

Yesterday's dregs
Vineyard's dead age,
Sun-frowned she sags
Lost for today,
I drink with her thirst
Tomorrow must pay.

Bitter her taste
Sweet was her mouth
Swallowed in haste,
Drunk was my hope
Dry, pale and full
Lost to all scope.

13th May 1992

GOLFER'S EYE

This non deception upon a green day,
A swinging satisfaction long denied
As bunkers with magnetic mouths halt play
Whilst sand-filled shots with swearing are applied.
There's business and a hundred things discussed
But life and death are only on the course,
Each hook and slice to rectify or bust
With inhibitions lost and gained by force.

Fierce rain and snow do nothing to prevent
The spirit of a golfer in full flow
When winning of a handicap event
To bask in clubhouse glory's afterglow.

How strange to even sacrifice one's soul
To knock a ball that further at a hole.

27th April 1994

BELLS OF WAR

Insidious the plot that drives the spirit
Destroys yet hides in chameleon shells
Inviting danger yet never near it
To inspire the ring of rhetoric bells.
Now hear the drums advance through distant fields
And feel the tears of blood roll down our cheek
For we know of little that hope's heart yields
When foes have cut our sight when love we seek.
Lion and the fox are one in panic
The chaser and the chased reverse their roles
Imposters both when fear drives calm to manic
Unrecognised their unrepentant souls.
But what know they who instigating law
Hear nothing of that knell from bells of war.

28th November 1996

SONNET TO DIANA

I was never sure of that smile till now,
It haunts me like an unquiet heart's refrain,
A lingering leaf on an Autumn bough,
A hidden tear lost in the weeping rain.
O knell that lulls you to a perfect sleep
As silent strangers resurrect your past,
How sad to never see that harvest reaped
Or watch the crown of protocol slip fast.
Was it this naive facade endearing
The sparkling spell beneath compassion's wand
Made us feel the simple good appearing
That fools have feared and wise men saw beyond.
Hope evergreen, your legacy of care,
Love caught in a memory's fragrant air.

10th September 1997

Ivor Vernon Smith

FORGOTTEN LIMBO
Sonnet to my son's coma

Hidden smiles, lost thoughts, or were you weeping
For all the freedom of reality
Behind locked doors in fate's chosen passage
As tortured eyes they left the day sleeping
Whilst faceless angels of your night would be
Your unfelt hope in heaven's sweet message.
Rest quiet from fear my son - no curses blamed,
Yours is the mystery in Morpheus' plot
An unheard hiccup from an uncleared throat
That fired the breathless, fevered heart untamed
Into a maelstrom's troubled twisting knot
Down, down to your castle's widening moat.

Now faith, her soothing oils have cleansed your sores
And answered prayers give all that love implores.

6th *January 1985*

SONNET TO SHIRLEY

There's little that I have not said before
Of this generated daily blessing
With your pure heart, yet deep I feel it more
Melting in those clear dark eyes, caressing
My inner self which you alone explore,
Treasures that no word could dream expressing

Your body's vision lingers evergreen
I kneel before your temple's perfect shrine,
It seemed as though the world had never been
Before my arms your slenderness entwined
Your face bore truth that I had never seen
As though the gods had gifted love divine.
It matters not what highs or lows there be -
You are my heart, my soul! my destiny!!

1995

UPON THIS APRIL DAY
A Wedding Sonnet

Upon this April day you turned and smiled
Across the memory-shaping aisle, where
Joy-filled a congregation rose, spring-styled.
Organ tremors embraced the truth-inviting air
Then honoured vows exchanged hope-laden hearts
That held these precious moments to rejoice
In unison that blissful trust imparts,
Confirming deep commitment in one voice.

Carriage and pair through fields of promise rolled
Past Chilham's Tudor beam and lattice-work,
A hedgerow blossom freshness calls, 'Be bold!
Fear not where past and future shadows lurk;
And may cherished pride her riches convey
Your finest dream upon this April day.'

14th March 1996

WIMBLEDON ECHOES

It is June, S.W.19 now,
The concourse throbs with expectancy's thrill
A world's hysteria focused on how
The ultimate tennis image in skill
Blooms for a fortnight when seeded a year;
Definitive ghost or merely sublime
Those Centre Court gods of the past appear
In a cathedral's ivy-clad echoing shrine
Where mellowed traditional flair's mystique
Lose hope-winning smiles in truth's drowning tears,
On green velvet stage for moves deft and sleek;
Euphoric Pegasus heart-lifting cheers
Rise somewhere between the crowd and the court,
A legend-filled dream in the guise of sport.

18th June 1996

PART III – Longer Poems

THE GIRL IN THE WOODS

Was she the nymph who danced in limpid springs,
Who held the answer to my seeking heart,
Encompassing all visions' mystery fair
Weaving with her gently fingered art
The starlit spell nurturing living dreams
Stealing through those tortured shrouds of doubt.

Are you a memory in fallen leaves?
Swirling past the torrid haze of youth,
Hellenic beauty as would the gods bestow,
An image for the frantic soul whose truth
Lies in the deepness of this silent wood
Yet saw not Winter through a Summer's growth.

How now, sweet temptress, did your soul conspire
To daunt this heart with liberated power,
Strength I alone would feel you consummate;
With sensuous touch you felt the growing flower
As truth did kiss the scorning petals' briar
Till surely I would know of beauty's glower.

Now turning to Narcissus' mirror
I so beheld an awesome inward sight
Of body Greek and countenance so fair
Did put to shade the sun's meridian light.
So sure the deep reality was formed
Pleasure-endorsed in vanity's delight.

What is this lens through which your beauty dawns,
Not, I dread, the dream of life's illusion
Fulfilling all those fantasies of form and art
Feeding this unto the soul's delusion,
Wondering the wondrous of reciprocated love
Lost in a hushed wood's Autumn glade bemusing.

A spectre from the conjured depths, time-pledged
In honest vein through sacrificial dust
From trauma on through blinded latency,
There nurturing an undenying lust
E'er ghosting past her pleasured innocence
To glimpse the dreamer's locket in sleep's trust.

And here within the dark'ning wood she came
And through her presence I did meditate
In studied measure from a calm repose
To bid of logic, yet to hesitate,
For what of logic and her offspring fact
That man would ever twist appropriate.

She drifted by yet not in vision's line
Whilst blending soft within the dawning grey,
It was as though a thousand hopes were born
And scattered 'cross the morn of fresh dismay;
Would for me this taunting cease forever
So I might melt with her in sweet array.

Fair temptress, pause to think alone of me
That we should meet and glow in sweet embrace
A multitude of yearning would you free
If I could kiss that untouchable dear face
To live no further than your heart, and draw
Angelic breath which fills your passing space.

Now time, what has been truly spent of thee?
Instead to greet the unresisting chance,
Guiltless waste when minds so positive act;
But not for me to justify this trance
If trance indeed it ever was when you
In beauteous truth did through the woodland dance.

I did become all you would ever wish
In daydreams from you cloud suspended,
Tormented Echo there abounding

Till silence on the wood descended
To chill the sun-spend sapling raw
Awakening to a fable ended

Yet ever onward would my spirit drift
Through rainbowed star-ways filled with spectrum art
As though the elements had lent their sky
A weeping sun compassion to impart
Upon the untold highs, cloud-crossed ere time
Had chanced to breathe in rhythm with fate's heart.

You sang of love and danced the elms with fire
Yet love nor fire was in your heart for me,
And though the woodland stirred as that sweet voice
Broke sharply now upon my reverie,
I cared not how the rudeness caught this mood,
Possessed was I with form and imagery.

Ageless as the envied air through which you pass
I see you rising from the dawning gloom,
And though I never kiss that mystic smile
For me my heart inhales on joy's perfume
Each time this bless-born sight rejoices so
Before the wonderment of perfect bloom.

Less purpose had I than the sparrow frail
In search of fresh grubs for the morn's repast,
For me the sight of that fair child was all
To nourish this my heart's impetuous fast,
For sure amidst the breathless boughs there lurked
A phantom darkened by the haunted past.

Yet what of time; her unforgiving eye
Sees all, 'tis said, though not care I nor will
There be for me one solitary doubt
These famished thoughts must need have of their fill
The imagery there, sylph-like gliding,
No matter what devouring hours do kill!

Was she the nymph who danced in limpid springs
Or wandering of the mind transcended
Escaping thus to this - seclusion's glade,
A self-willed prisoner, tree-defended,
This freedom sweet to peer through foliage brown
And hear soft strains of the song long ended.

Now rises the moon, and there 'cross the glade
A strange silence falls, a chill hand does seize
This twilight gloom with the ice-grip of dread
As I pause in the frail arms of naked trees,
While mist-drawn and pastward slowly she fades,
Girl in the wood on the late Autumn breeze.

5th February 1978

ODE TO THE SELF-EMPLOYED

They ask how it's going, you say very well
Though you know deep down that it's bloody hell,
With business not what you thought it would be
With those creditors threatening bankruptcy,
And the landlord pushing hard for his rent,
How little he knows that it's already spent
On luxuries like food and clothes for the kid
As today you drive at tomorrow, to skid
On unforeseen ice that formed in the night
When everything seemed to be going alright,
Till that dreaded postman turns down the drive,
Or a day's reprieve lending strength to survive.

It would take an army of men such as Freud
To unravel the minds of the self-employed
With the anguish and the apprehension
The cogs of strain enmeshed with tension,
Chasing the accountant every minute
Wondering whether he's dropped you in it,
Fearing lest the bailiffs swarm -
No limited company did you form;
Be sick never nor seek the dole
For that is played a devious role,
Dispensing with pride in the guise of maturity
Down on your knees at the Social Security.

Things, are of course, not always so grim
When the dog-paddling ceases and you learn how to swim,
Providing the wife can retain her sanity
And the bank still treats you with humanity,
As the scraps are whipped up with expenses all paid,
You can breathe with the breath you alone have made.

3rd March 1975

OLD RUPERT

Rupert through the city strode
With ostrich-proud and springing stride
His eyes were heavens up ahead
His lingering mind a hill behind
And all along and all around
Down bustling, lonely streets he stared,
Down lanes of stalls in cockney land
Where clipped vowels formed no wasted word
On Rupert striding through the crowd.
His presence was a shapeless thought,
A passing blank on reason's board,
A crossing wire held neutral taut,
The unfused terminals ignored,
For all around was lost in life
Multitudes toiling and eternal
By Rupert, gazing from his plight.

The dawn began to feel her pulse
Whose golden heart spread 'cross the square
As Rupert marched his unset course
And scattered pigeons everywhere,
He shrugged as Nelson turned his back
Whilst skipping to a gentle laugh,
Then to his pace gave measured check
Saluting at the Cenotaph.
A King and pauper was he both,
Speaker to the listening air
He led his subjects deep in truth
And opened Parliament each year.
Eleven chimes 'Big Ben you're fast',
I must say 'this is quite absurd,'
He checked it on an empty wrist
Then held the Changing of the Guard.

His garden it was Regents Park,
He chased dogs pissing up the trees,
Where often he would walk til dark
To peep at lovers through the leaves,
Then as his busy day was done
Old Rupert he would call the stars,
They were his family, every one
And ever lit his homeward paths.
The only creditors he had
Were drinks he owed, a pint or two,
When business men so smartly clad
Lived on credit's tightening screw.
Yes Rupert could have had all this,
But tripped down academic stairs
Since when he blew the world a kiss
A giant freed from city cares.

20th April 1981

STROLLED IN SILENT MISTS OF GREY

I strolled in silent mists of grey
Along the dark lane where my soul
In clouded dreams was borne from day,
And in the twilight there it stole
A glittering nightworth's bold array
To fly the earth from pole to pole,

And don the cloak that Styx had thrown
High from his tilting western perch,
Where in abandon time had sewn
A blinding patch to halt my search
Where deeper sight than I had known
Had glimpsed decay within that church

Wherein man knelt before his shrine
To sacrifice his perfect speech
For one last sip of bitter wine
Engaging all else than beseech
Mercy of the power divine
Whose parables denied his reach.

I fled the darkness in dismay
Though never would those thoughts dispel
That kneeling image of decay,
Nor ever would my tongue dare tell
Where rolled the silent mists of grey
In which my silent footsteps fell

22nd April 1975

NAKED RHYTHM

Paranoia drums the air
Fills time's frantic tempo
Drills a deepening bass,

See the unplucked heart-strings form
Frustration's hidden rhyme
Bursts forth blank verse crescendo

Yet ever losing time
Till sweet loves baton waves
A naked rhythm beat

Is drawn to nature's song
From now until the grave
Beneath blind, dancing feet

On rain-comprehending grass
Slaking deep an arid thirst
Gropes a sunward path

Through the fallen blossom
On a green-day magnet
Seeded from her past.

29th March 1993

BOLERO

Let me listen to your wily throat,
It seems difficult to perceive
Tomorrow may be your last attempt
At placing the straw before the wind.
Visions reveal little to my old sight,
A distant throbbing plays love's Bolero
And I feel that sensuous hand at large.
Gently the fingers flicker through the fire
The rhythm mounting the approaching strains
As a new cause for sweating begins
And the drums swell within my skull,
For now it draws a one-way sound;
Unending is the crescendo,
Unending from a lost beginning.

22nd February 1982

SUMMER LEGS

I never could imagine,
Beyond a wild thought,
What a climax in a sweating heaven
Would mean to my over-ripe childhood
I would dream of Summer legs,
Of settling old scores
With the teasers in the park,
Of consoling the near-raped virgins
Behind a noble facade
Self-seducing the green libido
With an untried Spring-drawn hand.

There were times when dying in bed
Frustration lay a nagging cancer
Eating through my puberty
Like a starving rat through cake;
Yet living through the night's reality
Dawn adjusted my cooling fantasy
Drew on the day-lusting skin,
Tempting a wealth of hypocrisy
From maturity's aching mould.

5th May 1982

SCORING

No one is certain
When the game started
Or who started it.
It just happened,
Like a crowd had gathered
And it was on,
Someone made up some rules
And everyone ran and kicked,
There was screaming
And a whistle was blown,
Sides were formed,
Goal posts erected
And a ball produced
Which looked the same to everyone
(About all anyone had in common)
Officials controlled the players,
The crowd controlled nothing
Especially themselves
A few thought it a good idea
To board up the goals
As if this life
Wasn't enough of a stalemate already,
Then someone moved the goal posts
And no one knew where they were meant to be,
It seems the only thing for certain
Whether player, spectator or official
If your aim be true or wild,
In order to score in this life
You first have to cross the penalty area.

7th April 1993

FURORE

There is praise in much abundance to test the open ear
The worthiness of which can ne'er be judged
By vanity's near-sighted claims, that smudged
A critic's eye, in sweet appraisal to a bold veneer.
There is much in retrospect to claim and justify
A cause (though caution be the solitary guide)
Starving through the bone the truth implied
Upon conceit's inviting ear to qualify
A place where praise cascaded like a blossom fall,
Denying yet the fruit from petalled bliss
Leaving Autumn's space to reminisce
On confidence and dreams and Summer's call.
Now, wild furore, on muted clouds begone!
Your fresh delight has waned, and love has won.

14th March 1977

TRUST

Trust a fool
Trust a wise man
But beware
The fool
Who thinks
He's a wise man

Trust the enemy
Trust a friend
But beware
The enemy
Who thinks
Like a friend

Trust in hell
Trust in heaven
But beware
The hell
That feels
Like heaven

7th May 1993

Ivor Vernon Smith

THE YELLOW SEA

Yellow-boned, the brittle waves are thrown
By youth, in unsuspecting dawn,
And with her gentle sips
Day-shy, the coy sun dips
To hold within dusk's margin
A lingering smile, submerging
'Neath an afterglow of tranquil bliss,
(To e'er fulfil day's promise)
For sallow waves a kiss,
Such warmth from which
Those tide-cracked lips could ne'er conceal;
The sea-bells tongue (salt blistered)
Alee of Hell, moon festered,
Harbouring yet the antidote, sea-shelling
A tidy oyster, born within her mould)
From the innards ocean rung,
Tolling from whose mercy all clear notion hung
Tear-drowned in the fear-pulled knell,
A hollowed rasp, a grateful well
Echoing deep in sallow days
God-strung in eternal praise,
Leeching faint the flesh of valour,
Scaling pigment from life's colour.
Noiselessly the tide has risen
In scorning wind's air-bent derision
That turned upon the glaciered calm
And cracked the ever graceful charm
To shed the minute of its load
And spur fresh sea horse, roller rode
Upon the saddled surf betraying
Naught but love's ride, there displaying
All the craft, therein denied
By brittle waves of ocean pride
That would in untoward displeasure

Flood the breaker's lockered treasure;
How swift they sink the yellow bones
Where men had dropped their rotting thrones
(Down where the green blood spilt it's past)
In darkest grotto's lusty moon.
Where brittle dreams were nightly hewn
From rocks of sin, where daily hardened,
The honest dream-work duly pardoned

2nd September 1975

Ivor Vernon Smith

THE BALLAD OF THE GREY & BLUE

Grey and blue, grey and blue
What does it mean to me and you,
When young Americans slew each other,
Father fought son, brother fought brother.

Grey and blue, grey and blue
Lost are the tears in the morning dew,
As mothers hugged men like children again
Their hearts too numb to feel the pain.

Sergeants shouting in the dawn,
Horses panting, sabres drawn,
Not for them to wonder why
What would dying justify

Grey and blue, blue and grey,
Sad colours blending in the fray,
Bayonets stabbing, rifles firing
Bodies trembling, spirits tiring.

Fighting with a fervour yet unmatched
This young America barely hatched,
Our lusty child to have its fling
Biting deep on the teething ring.

Bugles wail, day's slaughter done
Stained earth 'neath the setting sun,
Say your prayers, this starry night
Tomorrow may be your last fight.

Jackson, Sherman, Grant and Lee,
Good men all, but blind to see,
Battles won yet winners never
Rivers of blood that flow forever.

Passing days and passing years,
Pride hides everlasting fears,
Hate, oppression, how they last
Though Lincoln's hundred years have past.

John Brown one man they had to kill
Who had the spirit and the will,
Then half a million had to die
Beneath hell's darkening Autumn sky.

What justice in those Union graves
For breaking shackles of the slaves,
What price amendments of an act,
A treaty or a common pact.

Shiloh, Bull Run, dropping like flies,
Blind men screaming their battle cries,
Young boys writhing there in pain
Veterans swearing all in vain.

Jackson halted in Shenandoah,
Mustering troops now tired and sore,
With lightning thrusts and guns of thunder,
He split the Union lines asunder.

Slowly how the hour hand turns,
Marching whilst Atlanta burns,
Dragging feet to the welcoming sea,
Sealing a negro's right to be free.

A stumbling line for seven miles
Lost faces with forgotten smiles
"When will it end?" a trooper cried,
But nobody heard and nobody lied.

Now Richmond fell and all was lost,
Peace! but how to count the cost,

Ivor Vernon Smith

A piece of paper duly signed
Witnessed by God for all mankind.

Gone the bloodshed and the glory,
Historians try to tell the story,
Can words spell suffering, death and fear,
Deprivation's stolen tear.

Southern pride has flown today,
Johnny Reb has run away,
Banners gripped by stubborn hands
Scattered in the prairie sands.

Scapegoats there to lead the shame
The Confederacy would shoulder blame,
The world would hear and drink a toast
To the felling of the whipping post.

Could guilt be felt upon this shore
When Forefathers sowed the seeds of war,
Selling slaves to toil the field
For the white boss man to have his yield.

Congress offered to quench the thirst
Of the South who moved their black pawn first,
They lost the game, no more to do
But fight Apache and the Sioux.

Farewell Johnny Reb, farewell soldier blue,
The drums will ever beat for you,
The flutes will ever play your tune,
For that day when you grew old so soon.

June 1974

REASON'S RHYME

There was a stillness
Like the world had suddenly braked,
A numbness that no nerve
Would associate with feeling,
All order vanished
In the gloom of inevitability.
Even at this late moment
There still seemed a point
In recalling the idea
That life hadn't always been
An unmade bed,
A bucketful of crap
On the upturned face of humanity.
So for the last time
Let's all hold hands together
Drunks, slobs, perverts, queers
Any object of ridicule or fear
Nobody cares any more
(As if the bastards ever did).
All meaning meaningless
All Rhythm out of time
One last stab for old reason
We'll finish with a rhyme.

1988

Ivor Vernon Smith

A COMPUTER WEPT

A computer wept,
Programmed sorrow filled her face and crept
Into the digital day,
The pacemaker heart
Pausing for the clotted artery
Broke before the lies of progress
Pouring words of blood
In syllables of wrath
Upon gains turning worm.

Into the mighty lap
Sped the leading bunch,
Hysteria sweetly whipped
Her driven dust
As the crowd now ran the race
With the runners in the stands
And the starter pistol fired
As the loser broke the tape
And time's bullet hit the mark
And.......A Computer Wept.

ULTRA SENSITIVITY

Ultra sensitivity
Bears a cross of thorns
Down nightmare street,
A recurring penance
Unforgiving -
Yet ever compelling
In unproven satisfaction;
A gamble of hearts
Upon a mystic fortune
From a losing hand
Of Finite purpose;
Inflexible the choice
Savouring self indulgence
On suicide's cliff top
Drawn as a jealous lover
To deep suspicion
Of a chance remark
Turning the inward screw
To the nerve-ends of distraction.

1992

BROOKLYN BRIDGE

Funny thing, suicide,
Spending a lifetime
Reaching this point,
Yet pausing to make sure.

Are you savouring the moments.
Or is this just another chicken-out?

Jump! You bastard. Jump!
It's crazy when you're dead already.
God, how I envy you
This ultimate one-upmanship.

Free! Free! Bloody Free!

A passing thought, though,
(Perhaps on the way down) -

No one has the monopoly on misery;
Merely the choice and degree.

Have a nice day now,
Missing you already!

5th December 1983

APPRECIATION

Toil, you dreaded waster
Of art's fine precious space
When need in blindness begs.

From boredom's peril spare me
Who swims against a shallow tide
In drowning strokes displacement
To Winter's hollow shore,
Where wordless strangers roam the rocks
Dwell tight in cultured shells
Who hear the thundering ocean's mind
Yet fear the ripples at their feet.

Those ripples form entangled thought
Swiftly recede to form once more,
But waves like art cannot be taught,
They surge up unsuspecting shores
To anglers keen, who can be caught.

6th August 1984

Ivor Vernon Smith

THE CAVE
(Based on "Allegory of the Cave" - Plato's Republic

Compelled to stare at yonder wall
At darting shadow and fleeting image,
Inspired by leaping flames behind,
Objects move, the shapes are seen
But what opinion can formulate,
From such conjecture and fantasy.

But there is one in search of truth,
Who escapes and crawls from this dark cave
The climb is steep up rocks of slime,
Fall he must with few footholds
But emerging from that void of ignorance
To be blinded by the light of knowledge.

Slowly eyes attuned to dazzling glare
Of the mother sun at its zenith,
Now with mind and spirit nourished,
He heard a voice from the blackness below
And now began his grim descent
To the slaves of their environment.

With cautious tongue he filled their ears
With gems of wisdom he's acquired,
But imprisoned in their mind's dungeons,
The captive souls comprehended little
And rebuked the words not knowing why,
Yet electing him their King of Light.

THE LONGEST DREAM –
On My Father's Death

Old man, you lie there in your cot
The circle now complete,
I know not whether you care not
Nor if you breathe deceit.

Your limbs are twigs your hair is snow
Your wintered grief is born,
The memories flood in constant flow
To spill in eyes forlorn.

Conscience mine you twisted thus
Indifference to the air
And I am here to feel that trust
Behind the muted stare.

There was a time long ere this day
When deep in haste you came
And took my hand to lead the way
When pining did inflame

The passion dark in misery
Though not through fault you left
A child in loneliness to flee
Black nights, of love bereft.

Yet balance to this memory falls
As nights you drank away,
Corrupting all with drunken calls
And did my faith decay.

This son I brought to witness fate
Whose hand you clasp is mine;
The walls are yours to contemplate

Those days of song and wine;

Each dream is your reality,
Each utterance your shame,
Am I but here, therefore, to be
The sharer of your pain.

The dust-tongued bell does surely toll
In twilight's gentle close,
Old man I leave you to your soul
Whose misery you chose.

14th July 1977

BOGGED BLIND IN BULL

The world is full of bullshit, son,
From every angle you can view,
And this applies to everyone
Including me and you.

In each contemporary dwelling
Is bred a mind of glint and gloss,
And when full tongues of praise are swelling
Who really gives a bloody toss!

There's hope and deep sincerity
The medias' gifts drop in our lap -
We're all born to prosperity,
Now what a load of crap!

Man inherits his conditioning
Dumb and numb, to blind to see
The sinister implications -
This bullshit's in its infancy!

(When they admit that we're bogged-blind in bull
We'll hand on conditioning convinced to the full.)

10th December 1979

Ivor Vernon Smith

ONE MAN BAND

Before the crowd,
Slightly embarrassing all
Who wondered why
He was performing
This daily ritual
Or why they witnessed
In ghoulish curiosity
Ultimate independence
Of a deeply conceived fart
Wafting around their presence.

The music lied
From her bad memory
Inharmonious in thought
But that of discord
An elaboration of phrasing
Wallowing in lost ideals;
Let's stuff the day and listen,
Does anything really matter
As one more fall guy
Leaps into oblivion
Pulling his own strings
Deaf to his own cymbals
And the trumpet dirge
To a dead drum.

13th April 1994

THAT'S ALL

Close the lid I've had enough!
Never to repay those borrowed dreams
Never to know the outcome of schemes
I once began till life turned rough,
Never to clasp your dear soft hand
And breathe the fragrance of your youth
And skip the page of wisdom's truth
Weaving wonder's unplanned.

The world is closed. all business ceased,
Time's energy is overdrawn
The feet of fools are cramped and worn
A sea of tears has been released.
And I know not the perfect lie
To leave for you my epitaph
For should you know me you would laugh
If I left words to make you cry.

For I have dug a cynic's grave,
A ton of salt shall bear my name
Covering my shallow shame
Of bitterness that did enslave
My empty soul with callous stuff
That I had used in my defence,
And now at last no more pretence
That's all, piss off, I've had enough!

THE BALLAD OF JESSIE WHITE

I first saw the whore called Jessie White,
Falling out of a client's car,
The epitome of decadence
Staggering into the Brighton bar.

I don't know why but I followed her in
And everyone seemed to kiss her,
She smelt very strongly of cheap scent and gin,
There was no way that you would miss her.

Sitting cross-legged on a long bar stool
With her vultures circling around her
She pulled a cigarette from her lips
And blew a haze around her.

I stood transfixed in fascination
At this caricature before me,
Swigging her gin and pouting her lips
And choosing to ignore me.

She toyed with false hair in the mirror
Lost in her own reflection,
I was almost tempted to tell her
About that moon surface complexion.

She swapped each joke and shouted abuse
With remarks that were so profane,
And nobody heard and nobody cared,
Except me with my virgin brain.

The night wore on, but she stayed there perched,
A shrieking, uninhibited parrot
Till it dawned on me as she sunk their drinks
That they all hoped to bite at the carrot.

Jessie sang a lewd song and I felt myself blush,
It was hardly the twenty-third psalm,
She was bawdy and bad, gaudy and mad,
But I fell for her brassy charm.

She bellowed and roared all evening
Deep in the thick of the fray,
Politics, sex and religion
She always had plenty to say.

They drank and drank till it poured from their mouths
And they lost all reason and rhyme,
When turning to me she said, "Come on son,
Take me home and we'll have a good time."

I couldn't believe what was said at first,
So chaste and innocent was I,
Till she took my arm and clung like a leech
And we rolled 'neath the cool night sky.

She sang with great gusto and kicked a large cat,
As it's backside poked from a bin,
And somebody swore as a dustbin lid rolled,
But Jessie's voice drowned all the din.

We staggered into her dingy flat
And she told me to pour her a 'dwinky',
"This dress is too tight and it's starting to smell,
So I'll slip into something slinky".

She told me why she had brought me back,
"You're so different from the rest,
A picture of innocence, and I wanted some peace,
For I've got this pain in my chest!"

I suppose she had been lovely once,
Though this lechery was ending it fast,

Her profile was good and her bosom was full,
But the eyes, neck and cheeks couldn't last.

"They call me a slut, a bag and a whore
And I guess they are probably right,
But they know where to come when they're lonely and tired
On a wet and windy night."

I asked how she started this terrible life,
She replied, one thing above any other,
That her father seduced her when she was sixteen,
Then slept with her more than her mother.

"I had a baby once you know,
His father a choice from ten,
So I gave him away the very next day
And in six weeks was back with my men."

"Do you ever think of him?" I asked,
"Yes, often," came the reply,
"But I only grin and knock back the gin,
For life is too short to cry!"

We talked through the night and she drank like a fish,
Till I started a fit of yawning,
She said, "I've never felt so relaxed before",
As the first light of day was dawning.

All of a sudden she clutched at her throat
And fell in a fit on the floor,
Choking and writhing, she cried out aloud,
"I'm a goner this time for sure!"

I phoned for an ambulance and did what I could
To increase her chance of survival,
They tore through the streets, but her pulse had few beats,
And Jessie was dead on arrival.

The Whole Slice

A few hours was all I had known her
Yet deep was the effect on me,
I wondered why she had touched me so
Was it drink or just chemistry?

I saw the doctor later that day,
To ask him the cause of her death,
"Her liver was addled, the heart took the strain
And her lungs they just ran out of breath.

I told him I hadn't slept with her,
At which he seemed very pleased,
"I've examined these women for many a year
But never saw one so diseased."

"One can't do these things to the body,
It just cannot be so abused,
It would seem as though she had wanted to die,
The way it had been so ill used."

Could it have been that she hated this life?
But continued to wear a facade,
For it struck me the brief time I knew her
That she seemed to be trying too hard.

They chipped off that mask of cheap makeup,
And with eyes agog I did stare,
For instead of remains of great beauty,
A wizened old hag lay there.

I told her landlord that she was dead,
"Poor old Jessie!" he declared,
"Not bad company, and tried hard in bed,
Providing one was too drunk to care!"

I stood soaked with rain at the funeral,
Whilst her coffin slid down that hole
Prying alone, for nobody cared

For bad Jessie White and her soul.

Then I called in the bar and told them
Of the peace that Jessie had found,
And nobody heard and nobody cared
For that baggage who lay in the ground.

Was this a life that was wasted?
Or was it just meant to be,
At least she had given some pleasure
Be it by choice or by destiny.

May 1974

THE SCRIBE

Was it written?
The future of mankind,
On tabloids of the mind,
Etched in the brain's crust,
Seen, yet unperceived,
Through mists of time
In forests of learning,
The sun's truth
Endeavouring to peer through
The foliage of misconception,
Tears of dew forming
On sad Autumn leaves,
Dampening the ground
Where Summer's bare feet trod,
Clouding judgement,
Till the axe of courage
Removes all doubts,
Hacking its way
Through fear and prejudice,
Revealing a fearless sky,
Unafraid of its stars
And destiny's soul

1974

ONE BACKWARD GLANCE

Turn not complete;
One backward glance
It will suffice
A gentle yardstick
To a questioning past,
Then forward point,
Stand not aghast
For what is done
It may return,
A spectre dark
'Neath reason's bridge
Where sunken lockers
Wait with jaded hope,
Treasure trove, love-dealt
Beyond all wealth
Buying up unhappiness.

No false starts,
Keeping in the right lane
Leading contentment's field.
Ever in sight
The winning line,
No need, the lap of honour -
Though, maybe just.......
One backward glance.

29th July 1984

JUST A THOUGHT

Hindley, Sutcliffe -
Headlines, biographies,
Fred Watson
Samaritan and Philanthropist -
Nothing!

Rainham Churchyard, Kent,
Local vicar for twenty years
Lies buried
Next to Jack Keene
Murderer and rapist,
I wonder if the worms
Ever discriminate.

If any of this is of significance to you,
Then you are as lost
As I am!

28th April 1993

JANUARY'S BRIDE

January's bride,
Gliding headlong through the tempting aisle
Pew-dotted in snow dust observance
Forgetful of the warning banns
She, the love child of fate's chill
Harmonious with the consummate urge
Unsuckled in lust's bosom,
He, an unrivalled suitor for the final vow,
A belated memory clutching the pulpit's fallen words
Syllable glanced from acoustic grasp,
Together, pledging their troth beyond all denial,
The ice-spun veil melting 'neath the dogma's fire
Till naught but shallow sockets held our truth,
And we, witnessing with neat, forging hands
The naked Winter's document
Sealed forever in the stained virgin eye,
Grope in feverish haste, the snow dust confetti.

12th June 1975

FOOLS ELEGY

My heart is in the gutter
And my mind is in the clouds
And when I speak I stutter
And my sight is tearful shrouds.

There are no stars to guide me
No sun to bless my path
No warmth I feel inside me
When flames lick bright the hearth.

Once I hung on wisdom's thread
Dangling on pretention's words
Till culture raised her mocking head
To quote the meaning I had slurred.

The most I am remembered
Is when a weaving thought
In some corny old September
In a mellow web is caught.

1992

GEOMETRICALLY OPPOSED

There are those
Whose minds remain but surface scraped,
Narrow in forward clutching angles,
Equilateral definitions bound
In knowledge frowned indolence,
Bearing sullen logic
Brow locked in vain
Upon a graph-peaked world
Of T-square rationality

There are those
Whose anxious pencils
Flit with nimble accuracy
Cross-warped drawing boards
Paper worn, ruler grooved,
Stale dimensions of tradition
Sky-housed on cloud footings,
Climbing to the utmost zenith
On a narrowing apex.

There are those
Geometrically opposed
To diverse forms, standard set
Before their contemporary vision,
Filing acute objectives,
Wrapped obtuse pleonexia
Word neat in glossy folders,
As only such misrepresentation
Will ever be so contained
Within a decreasing circumference.

24th April 1975

DEPRESSION'S DUST

Five inches tilled instead of two
Before Depression's dust she blew
To spin their soil 'cross callous skies,
One more American dream gone awry
Westward drawn in '87
They raced the prairies unborn heaven
Where there amidst the passive earth
Hope-powered sinew staked its worth.
Green grew the dollar late that Spring
Prosperity's bell did clearly ring
From triumphant peel to disaster's knell
Whilst the helpless earth she bore man's hell;
And all along old nature knew
Five inches tilled instead of two.

17th March 1978

REBELLION

Transferring drama in the mind
To action of a varying kind,
Compelled at last to make a stand
And grip the tyrant's whipping hand.

This torture and self-sacrifice
With tongues too tied for good advice,
With ears too burnt by blaze of scorn,
Those early hopes that seemed forlorn.

What is a man but one more soul,
To fill a space or play a role
And touch the warm walls where he's tied,
But not to lock the door of pride.

No love where there is domination,
But dread for this abomination,
Where doffed cap hides a raging torment,
An independence lying dormant.

1973

COULD I WITHIN A TRAUMA WRITE

Could I within a trauma write
Repression's deep and sorry thorn
And on my desperate bow draw back
To aim my subject to the night
And dream a rhymed and metered dawn.

In symbol-glittering starry air
Aloud I read the thoughts displaced
On unthumbed page's silent plot
And turned my fatalistic ear
From medleys of unsung grace.

When once he fell on perfect ground
There chilled the ghost down from his throne
Craving those warm bones, dusk denied,
Hovering, moon-held, by night's mound
To recite hell's epithetic groan.

Is this the man I have become?
A shallow hoverer in sleep's scar
Sustaining darkness, where all light
Has spread time's chapter since page one,
Riding high illusion's star.

Was there in life to pre-suppose
One notion that the pen would meet
Reality and the soul as one
And reap each pleasure day proposed
Through latent traumas yet discreet.

Deny thy image, sacred child,
Thine is the Kingdom hell has born,
Time is the book, love is the word
Lusting death's virgin so reviled,

Cocooned in the wisdom, mother-warm.

7*th* January 1976

AUTOPILOT

Visionless, strapped breath-light
In numbing clouds where untouched
By lessening time the tranquil space
Plots a past from a passing present.

And Kings and cities fall from love
Whose perch has swung in mystic mood
And so forever does it swing,
Witnessing lust's inevitable move.

The smile of Summer lingers yet
Though for what purpose, when comes the dark
And blinds but deeper still the tongue
Interceding thoughts of season hope.

Long is the firing of the drums
And with each shot the drummer falls,
Batons raised against the wind
Rhythm charging to a perfect end.

So drifts the abstract of the earth
As abstract goes the passing life-
Lost in the void of passing thought;
Unmanned the scenario of each plight
Spun blind in the path of a giant foot.

27th July 1982

Ivor Vernon Smith

WINTER 'GAINST MY CHEEK HAS BRUSHED

Winter 'gainst my cheek has brushed
So raw and sharp to breathe upon
This prone, stark face yet scarlet flushed
From Summer world, now gone, now gone.

Winter 'gainst my cheek has chilled
Chafing with a coarsened hand
And blemish countenance so fair
Indentures of cruel seasons brand.

Winter 'gainst my cheek has shed
A glowing tan's reflected youth,
For what hid I on hoar-frost night
One more concealment of the truth.

Winter 'gainst my cheek has cut
Eternal channels flowing blood
'Cross weathered face of countless storms
Alone now shivering in fire's mud.

Winter 'gainst my cheek has swept
Brown flaking leaves in late surrender
That rode in hope on snow bound gusts
Oblivion blown each last offender.

Winter 'gainst my cheek has held
A lamp to things I never saw
Nor ever dreamt in August glory,
For Summer is no more, no more.

1975

WHAT'S HER NAME?

Whatever happened to what's her name,
I think she was pretty,
Though I know she was lame.

She had a slight squint though it never distracted
The magnetic gazes
That cruel leg attracted.

More sympathy gained if she had been blind
Or deaf to foul names
As she hobbled behind.

At night she would cry on her mother's breast
To wash away sorrows
As she stood each day's test.

At school she was ever the teacher's pet
Trying to impress
Yet lost in regret.

That she couldn't be stupid or play the fool,
For without this redemption
She would surely lose all.

I remember her once at a New Year's dance
Embarrassing each partner
Who dared take a chance.

Postponing the moment when she would arise
And her twisted limb
Met bewildered eyes.

Many an eye would turn where she sat
With her mind in a turmoil

When they came for a chat.

Where did she go to, What's her name,
After her party
When nobody came.

1974

THERE'S SIMILE AND METAPHOR

There's simile and metaphor,
Five syllabled, with which to play,
There's little purpose what they're for
When meaning's all one need convey.

There's bracketed in prose and verse
An afterthought, a passing line;
There's emphasis in that tub-thumped curse
And context-swearing is divine -

When unmixed premise creams a truth,
Infinity her circle turns
And dwells not on the dream of youth,
No fevered candle ever burns.

And in the melting leaves time's form,
No sweet imagining would last
Which would the spirit's longing warm,
For is not 'now' the future's past.

There's simile and metaphor,
Blind depths philosophies propound;
Pretentious mystics pace their floor
With naught but feet upon the ground.

12th May 1980

GUTTER

There's a comfort
In the gutter
Beneath contempt
Tucked well in,
No one knows you're there
Or if they did
They wouldn't care
Pavement vibrates
Neurotic feet pounding
The day's rhythm
Not for me hiding
In my chosen nadir
My sole aspiration
To peer above the kerb
At the two-way
Cul-de-sac
And when it rains
A niche within a niche
Down the drain.
I can live with rats.

28th July 1993

WHEN

On the one hand
Ignorance

On the other
High technology

In between
A forgotten heart

Leisure decays
Indifference dawns

Knowledge frowns
Turns her head

Yawns and stretches
See the hands are parting

Nevermore to clasp
And darkness breeds

Malignant power
Across the cells of space.

Ivor Vernon Smith

THE PARTNER

There is of all ingredients
In the recipe for life,
But one main thing - obedience
In the tolerance of a wife.

A cool clear understanding
Of the cards when they are dealt,
When not to throw the hand in
No matter what is felt.

To withhold deliberation
Drawn by opponent's bluff
And to avoid obliteration
When the kitty seems enough.

And should a change of game require
That she must be the banker,
To play not with a mean desire
And pay devoid of rancour.

Wits sharpened by the winnings
As the stakes once more are raised,
Remember poor beginnings
How smallest gains were praised.

Chips are counted, you have won,
The losers homeward weave,
Tonight you held a winning run
Tomorrow you may grieve.

And so, my love, hold fast
Lay deep in blissful slumber,
Yet not forgetful of the past
With a spine that ached with lumber.

1974

THE FINGER ON THE TRIGGER

The finger on the trigger
Trembles at the pulse,
Squeezes from the brain,
But for one moment holds the blame;
Points a silent course.

The silken sand that parts the rocks
Runs through the pulsing tide
Choking on love's pool,
Thickens the coursing swell,
Drowns on raping blood.

The wreck upon the moving shore
Twists a creaking spine,
Splintering each trauma
Plotting an ageless drama,
Marooned from reason's rhyme.

The finger beckons through the dark
Points the way of men,
Prods a bloating belly
In vain, to shape the jelly,
Beckons youth again.

The finger on the trigger
Shapes the burning sand;
Bungs the wrecking hole
Propping an unkissed pole
Above the flinching land.

LISTEN, MY LOVE

Listen, my love,
To my aching eyes
So often with exaggeration
Have I played down
With my inadequate tongue
The uncut words
From this mine of dull diamonds
Now for me
But one thing remains
That you see in these
My time-weathered sockets
One untarnished sparkle
Containing all yearning
And the fever of adoration
That long ago dried
On these pride-bitten lips.

TRADITION

Pulse rate quickens,
Eyes moisten,
The spine burns,
For what?
Empire building,
Each brick a life
Laid down by order,
The mortar a mixture
Of flesh and blood,
Pointed with bayonets;
Wave your flag, my son
Cheer each tank and gun,
You never knew
How much was lost
Of life's currency,
As it was poured
Through stained fingers,
Spit and polish
Now a mindless answer
To our hollow birthright,
For this proud mansion,
With leaking roof
And shallow footing
Was built on treacherous ground.

November 1973

AN ANT IN THE WILDERNESS

What is a man from a hill-top high
But an ant in a wilderness scampering by
Along shallow furrows of grim self-respect
Each wide-eyed hypothesis never cloud flecked;
That ego corrupting the mystification
Surrounding words steeped in justification
For deeds which meant naught in the final analysis
But forgotten ideals in a lost mind's paralysis.
Ever the hunter who seeks human prey
With a bait of forgiveness dangling away
On that line of compassion where well spent resistance,
Succumbs to the power of fate's deadly insistence,
Could he not see in that bid for the sun,
The cooling perspective he needs for life's run?

21st May 1976

EN PASSANT
Be it Heaven or Hell - all is in passing.

En passant, their King to slay
Yet not to self-confess nor gloat;
The mouthing mind to grip and play
Thought's teeth upon their lusting throat.

Across the board of sea and earth
They see the chequered spirit fly
Apart, yet close as death with birth
As tide-worn shores run fever dry.

Thundering clouds they pause unswept
Infesting but a man-filled sore
Forgotten as a dream that slept.
Blindly passing 'Go' once more.

Comes the mystic leap unchecked
Pawns of courage fill their square
Chasing Gods in vessels wrecked
By unseen time and unfelt care.

Steep the pulpit sways and topples,
A life-long sermon stumbles by,
Wading through the mocking ripples
Upward to the cross-filled sky.

Earthly shadows shape night's face
Devils circle round their moon,
Starlight weaves a midnight lace,
Upon time's endless racing loom.

Deeper flow the floods of Spring,
Seeds drown upon the gulping wave,
Brave tongues are drawing on the sting,

Word cargoes fill a season's grave.

Doubt's twilight fills her pensive hills
Though fever dawns each era new,
Fresh knowledge honing lightning skills;
Unchanging with the space time grew.

Sleep pours forth oblivion's rain
(Freedom's secret deep illusion)
Bears no promise but the pain,
Forms her pattern through confusion.

File the gaping past their ruin,
Built to endure the test of lies;
Sword of trust is left pursuing -
Through walls of light - the passing eyes.

8th May 1985

FOOLS IN THE SUN

These the drifting denim strangers
In non-conformist uniform,
Strolling past the hot news of yesterday
And the shrinking shadow of parenthood,
Finally surrendering to the young fools
Who thought that all they ever did
Or had ever done was playing corpses
In the dead grass among the litter bins,
At home with the brown banana skins,
Sitting in the tiresome sun, too hot to breathe
Too tense to dream, all words dried up;
No script to recognise through the blurring page.

So on the denim strangers drift,
On to the fairground mania,
Past the dead fools who know their place,
(far from the carousel syndrome,
Far from the manic dipper)
On through the noisy smell
Of all that is nothing, that drifts
With them that is part and whole
Of the blindness vital
To the young fools passing.
And the old fools passed.

7th August 1983

FIGHT!

Hell has burst between my ears
A devil's sun had scorched the sky.
Undetected come the fears
Where once deluded hope did lie.

Spell my manner, spell my need
With words enflaming, trauma-lit,
Race the night on death's dark steed
And watch time's star-stitched pattern knit.

No beacon flame held warning
Fate's nod nor destiny winking,
I woke a nightmare dawning
Day's cup of misery drinking.

Bitter eyes reveal the curse
That poured this evil on my head,
Hearing half the world is worse
Is scant solace when will lies dead.

If life's problems build our strength
So shall it be for those that cope,
Trouble-free in endless length
And I will wallow in my scope.

When others joy is gleaming
Sadness she weeps with no respite.
Like ice her vapour steaming –
Perhaps my norm could be this fight!

7th August 1996

INSOMNIA DESPERANDUM

Dusk's old neurosis building
Shadows of circumstance renewed
On night's fearful edge unwelcomed
Where exhaustion hides locked
In desperate perception
From day's smouldering afterglow,
Numb-fingered scaling stress mountain.

Now dark-heightening sounds close in,
Hammering clock, thundering car,
Nagging wind on rattling pane;
Conscience churning, prayer redeeming
Passive past-gripping vision
Where no calm area awaits,
No escapist niche for comfort.

How short the night, how long the hour
That fills each thought or movement
With wild frustration's non-respite,
Each fresh position's novelty
Short-lived beyond persuasion
Till comes dawn's dreaded sounds,
And day's fierce ambush begins.

7th May 1998

BEGGAR

See the beggar asking for spare change –
What does this mean – spare change.
If I was to die on the spot
Or had no further use for money
Only than something would be spare.
How can it be otherwise?
Let us not knock down bricks of pride
Built on amoral footings
As we pass on, comfort-bound,
Embarrassed into politeness
Draped in clichés stale cloak,
Leave his spit on your boot
To further polish security's gap
Ever widened by fear and conscience.
Turn the page on his no-matter book,
That cage is locked no matter what,
Turn up the heating, bugger the cost
How is it our fault people are lost.

In the doorway after dark
By the lamplight counts his take
Slides into a cardboard shell
Another day's humiliation done,
Whether we give or refuse
A passive or aggressive plea
The twenty pence we would not miss
Is earned by stifling shame's cruel tear,
And though our hands may never touch
Deep down we can smell the fear.

15th May 1998

A MOMENT HELD

From the pilot's cabin Gatwick bound
With vision clear and perfect height
I though no matter where one travels
There could never be a finer sight
Than Portland Bill upon your left
To the Seven Sisters on your right.

I gazed out on the patchwork quilt
That spread a lush green bed below
And through an English eye perceived
A heritage to make me glow,
For this was mine against all odds
From fate's hand tossed, a precious throw.

Peaks pierced the cloud tops far below
Our purring seven-four-seven,
Yet no sight could compare for me
Than that between Kent and Devon,
A moment held of all we own
Between the Isle of Wight and heaven.

The past's horizon vanished
Into another yesterday,
What was our experience really
But a foreign novelty's display
When blind pleasure shook our balance
Regained on that September day.

Now when I taste the storm of life
And chaffing winds bay at my plight
I think about that calm blue day
That showed me England clear and bright
When Portland Bill was on my left
And the Seven Sisters on my right.

24th September 1996

Ivor Vernon Smith

IN STARK SUBSIDENCE

I dug the frozen earth that morn
And though my feet
Were so entrenched with clay
And the east wind chilled my reason
I thought, why me
To fill the drabness
Pursuing an unrewarding drudgery
With relentless nerve and sinew,
When others, colouring their canvas
In warmth and splendour
Holding brushes in an unrealistic grasp,
Painted all purpose with pleasure's vision
Devoid of dark subsidence
In the decaying depths of uncertainty,
Turning upon me for sweet solace
When the palette wept
Beneath the flooding convergence
Of an over stirring hand
Lost in neurotic avarice
Of the drained knuckle,
Whilst I, lost to the high world,
Dug deeper my introversion
Sketching doodles by the forkful,
And raked my progress
Across another ice-filled trench.
How weather drawn and limp was I
As the skeleton of forgotten anguish
Lying a'gangling on his puppet joints,
A land fish challenging each earthy swell
In many layered time,
Harbouring a kingdom of afterthought
In the Triassic lesson, ancient and modern,
Bearing in a ruptured fin
All dread within the latest movement

When claw and fin held fast
And death crept through her indolent flesh
Swallowing a lifelong feast
Of unrepentant decay
And I, drunk from the dew of my forefathers,
Flung the last sobbing mourner from my grave.

30th January 1995

Ivor Vernon Smith

APOLOGY

Not only can I never
Feel your dark pain
Hasten your judgement
Taste your chagrin,
So can I never touch your grief
Balance your nature
Do more than offer
A spineless conscience,
A mindless hand.

When all dear time is borrowed
Drawing closer
A future's credit
Kiss not my eyes
They should have noticed
Where you have been
Calming my agony
Spilling my passion,
My frantic path –
Your measured tread.

Not only can I never
Repay the debt
I owe your love
So can I never
Redeem my unworthiness.

11th June 1996

THE STUBBORN DAY

There's a weakness
Like a virus
Spreading with an overpowering blindness,
Suppressing growth,
Repressing desire,
Clutching at dead twigs
Like an overheard innuendo,
Means nothing yet everything
To the uninitiated ear,
Yet waning in up-hill strength
In the face of compromise.

When as a child
I suffered from spite
Which I nurtured through recognition,
There seemed no retaliation.
So began my stubborn day,
A stalemate of perpetual check
Licking the dried wounds
Of my sullen impasse,
Striving to plumb no further depths
Yet wallowing in pride's morass –
Maturity's impostor!

13th February 1996

IVY-CLAD TRADITION

Ivy-clad tradition dawns
Dwelling in a mauve-green mist
Of memorable euphoria
Where shriek, roar and grunt
Reveal the moment's frantic mind.
Yesterday's idols drain renewed sweat,
Heave the message their legs cannot answer
Blind to being Kipling's 'impostors',
Only the yearning their ego demands
Seeing a clear Wimbledon sky
Through young clouds of effortless moves
Pounding toward victory ousting
Old pretenders from their crumbling thrones
As they in turn will suffer
Through unseen weakness and design.
Soon fresh rackets swoop and drive
And another media's dream awakens,
Precocious, endearing beauteous
Who can envisage what awaits
Beyond the Mecca's sunset
So turns the annual fortnight tap
Quintessentially English
They gorge upon their strawberry day
Yet inviting the cream of the globe
Stripping inhibition bare
To win hearts, trophies and fame,
And should failure loom, dream on,
To the ultimate stage return
Where the ghostly spaces once were filled
By illustrious style and flair.
Strange Eastern European names tongue twist
The commentator's clarity,
Fans clutching at instant appeal
Scream in extrovert anonymity.

Then all is done and shadows lengthen
On the Centre Court's hallowed ground,
The final applause fades
Into another year's oblivion,
A wilderness of exploding dreams;
And Ivy-Clad tradition yawns.

30th January 1995

SECOND GENERATION

When men were old and youth was lost
A time between the war and hype
I tolerated father's whim
For he alone knew what was right,
And when that goodness overflowed
It was not learning that remained
But knowing one of us bore truth
And most of what he spoke was shite.

I never thought one could resent
The patted back and well shook hand
But now I wallow in my stew
To stir in haste with gas marked high,
And yet on balance there must be
Respect for blind intention's bow
When aimed with power the arrow long
Fell short below trajectory's sky.

Conditioned therefore to endure
Not asking for nor carrying why
They live at credit's open door
Unlocked with caution by our need,
When ceasing to accept our place
Where once society hid its dreams
We set the rot within quiet slumber
Awakening to a nightmare's greed.

How strange the memory's failing
When seeing old mistakes reborn
By sharp, impetuous design,
We so condemn their wild advance
Upon convention's bastion
With time's face turned by guilty hands
Long ere they stormed our quiet breach.

As though this earth was spun by chance.

Were they perplexed when being taught
Those fine ideals we thought were just
Yet in transference of the Word
They must with fresh, objective hearts
Have contemplated how and why
The errors in established growth
Had spawned a deep malignancy
From which integrity departs.

We gave their complex years to dwell
Oedipus and Electra formed,
Then drew the screen on Psyche's trap
Held taut in that repressive net,
And when they showed no fortitude
To dark temptation's hidden plot
We taught them how to remember
Full knowing they would just forget.

They have no past to recollect
But infantile comparison,
No link on inhibition's chain
That drags the ageing ball of life,
Theirs is a kind of promised freedom
A paradise in credit set
That we bestowed with downcast eyes
So they in turn endured the strife.

When youth inherited spent power
Like spark to tinder, flame to ash,
A sin scorched trail was sure to spread
Till fine ideals so deeply set –
Were turned into a subtle trap
With continuity's bait hung sweet
On which those gullible mouths would feed
Gorging with trust unable to vet.

Born to accept conditioning
Seeking to create destruction,
Morality her rights are waived
Their blind technology thrusts and parries
At our defenceless old logic
All credence wanes to powerless dark
Like a switched off sun reborn
Lights their way yet never tarries

When empires fell and states were born
They lingered in the frozen sky
And stared upon the static wastes
Then turned the fresh earth with their plough
And spun a democratic top
Than wobbled to a final rest
Beneath the jack boots crushing step
Till Freedom's Spring fell from her bough.

Inherent in a lost belief
Through raw Neanderthal passing
A multitude of trust was laid
Upon successive passive heads
So when the philosophic breast
Bared before a new dimension
The power grew soft and yielded so
Old reason's weave had missed her threads.

Egyptian, Roman, Greek and Turk,
Through their centuries handed on
A civilised endorsement's pledge
That all would progress through the line
With necessary blinding vows
For in foresight all was seen
And never sense quiet warning sign.
Then we would not on hindsight draw

And so I grow my father's guilt
Established in the perfect ruins

Practising my indoctrined faults
To add the current ingredient
Drawn from the well of tradition
This recipe of mine and now
A pinch of modern seasoning –
Technological expedient.

I wonder why it all began
This driving to a hidden goal
Of aiming at a non- return
A subtle twisting fact,
Yet this is probably the way
Not all a man is meant to die,
A glimmer of a thought will live
Passed on for childhood to react.

6th August 1996

Ivor Vernon Smith

THE GIRLS OF AUTUMN

The faded brow, a deadlock on the gloom,
Gentle naped the slender neck bends
Swanlike 'neath a golden mantle
Soaked by sweat of the morning musk
Fear ridden on a scarlet dawn.

She calls her maiden prayer
Across the back glade of the memory's copse
And duly settles for a semi-echo
Caught in tired branches yawning their arms worth
In air patterned doodles of plan less art.

Leaf-light her anaemic feet did tread
The mist earth side of gaping heaven,
Whilst she descending, enveloping all
Within her endless span
Damp clung to Summer remnants.

How falls the ruin in its latest hour,
Dire need to bargain with dew pearls
Reflecting untold promise in sparkling guise
Ere donning cruel and callous cape,
A faceless hood denying sight.

Did she once drift on balmy eves
Across those richly nurtured vales
Casting with permissive joy
The lengthening shadow of her smile
To turn and see the world drift by.

And when the moon-kissed lake
Had settled in its shingle bed
Bidding waiting clouds to douse the light,
Could tepid touch be ever felt

Beneath a frigid calm that night.

Where did the rustic crossroads form
On latent highway's winding course
Glimpsed unobserved 'twixt birth and bloom,
Lost to glazed eyed maturity
Unformed shrouds of naivety.

What vision there did form
Cow-dazed in splendour from the light
Of meridian skies; on bracken bed to lie
And trace the spirit sketches
Across the cloud-framed sky.

To kiss the gentle fern
That waved its cooling wand,
A magic rhythm through the haze
Of cluttered imagery ever found
On pride's pretentious, narrow ground.

High ridden on precocious strains
A lush green melody,
Hanging from dull bough,
Withstanding yellow, searing eye
That probed above the leafy hid to pause
Whilst failing sight might stake a claim.

From blessed purity's untrodden path
A jaded jacinth, impatiently kicked
Beneath youth's dusty rut,
As passions thrusting thorn
Lingered in the pallid flesh.

Winter's latency sprung to life
In the well of Spring and Summer's glare,
Yellow-green to yellow-red
Bitter sweet to mellow rare
And on to Autumn's deepening spread.

Unyielding was the sturdy oak
Till lightning, wind and thunder rain
Combined, conspired, so to provoke
The branch to snap with pride and pain
Which swaying willow could ne'er invoke.

No more things as they would seem to be
Ignore not drab reality.
Awaken, rise, fear not the dawn
To pray before your fading star
And thank the Lord you came thus far.

Blossom forth, you girls of Autumn,
Cocoon-stripped shadows fill your wake,
Stand you tall and look beyond
The pale of childhood bliss and sorrow,
Shrivelled leaves upon the lake.

29th March 1975

SUSPICION'S COVER

Slowly we close day's book
Circumspect, heavy with neurosis,
What has been achieved, learnt,
Left undone, forgotten.
What does it matter,
Is there really cause for concern
As a new book opens on the morrow
With a new memory
And a fresh set of ideals,
New chapters with unexpected endings,
The odd new trigger word
Firing a little current knowledge
Soon to be overlooked, like fashion
Euphoric with freshness
Yet ageing in first impression
From its blind conception,
Like mankind, an institution
Established for inconsistency
And a continuing lack of durability
As the book of suspicion,
Prepared for the new grey dawn,
Is opened again in haste
As it was ever meant to be.

24th September 1996

SYRUP

So mighty arm how will you stir
When all the sinew for your power
Is numbed and powerless as the grave
Where none but chosen spirits cower.

How sweet the thickening fancy flows
Within love's fast and fickle tide
It is forever on the ebb
That flows space high and shoreless wide.

When will we know that moment sweet
That touches on the nerve of greed
To vomit from a bloated gut
And so admit beyond our need.

No! We are the pigs of squalor
Who gorge when fairness should suffice,
Cannibals on fellow syrup
That one would dare not sacrifice.

16th July 1998

ONE EDGED SWORD

Is this our dependent shield?
Law-contaminating justice
Breathing quiet in naivety
Synonymous in word alone
Our principle yardstick
Guided by the belief of acceptance
Delivered by a purring pedantry
Thickly spread by judgmental drone
Primitive our civilised state
Is numbed by the Christian one-edged sword
Hacking deep on unhealing trauma,
A 'got at' witness unprotected
Defending a noble faith
Drawn by duty's harsh conscience
Through lawyer-groomed expertise,
A wordsmith's ploy unsuspected

Discrimination loses sight
Upon the dim, grey threshold's
Minor or a major cause
Where notoriety kicks the day
With giant-footed insolence,
And whilst the slate still licks her bruise
The victim digs a silent grave
Our system withering in decay
And I know not (nor ever will)
Why this unfair weapon exists
Allowing justice to smile on the crossed palm
That presses the bias to the scales
When loaded rhetoric explodes
On the nervous, undiscerning ear
Finally bending for 'yes or no'
That fear-contrived a 'truth' unveils

10th July 1996

LONDON EYES

Up the A2 west of Eltham
From Shooter's Hill to Greenwich Park
We draw upon East London's lungs
Out on the fresh kite flying Heath,
Open Suburbia wide and free
An urban slum's wide verdant margin,
Regency to late Victorian
With plagued remains laid deep beneath.

The Old Kent Road whose grimy face
Is never washed nor shaven clean,
Through New Cross on to Bermondsey
A disillusioned first impression
Of civilisation's masterpiece
Where squalid streets and high rise flats
Lead through nothingness on to nowhere
Reflecting all our old depression.

These ever crowded lonely streets,
(The population of Australia)
A cosmopolitan melting pot's
Magnet of expectancy drawn
Past cold graffiti plastered walls
Where culture dyes her mixing bowl
With hell's ingredients dearly bought
From currency of a begging dawn.

Fish filled air at nostrils clinging
Before another Billingsgate day
And so to apprehension's gloom
As the silent city holds its breath
Whilst bankers, brokers, merchants rush
Across the groaning bridge packed morn.
For some, ambition soon fulfilled,

For others ever hastening death.

Trainee cabbies learn "The Knowledge"
Through the dense maze of suburbia
From Colliers Wood to Hither Green
Or St.James's Street to Finsbury Park
No greater task could one be set
Than this definitive A to Z,
This great metropolis mighty sprawl
On which no faint heart should embark.

Piccadilly her strobe-filled night
Holds decadence with carefree will
A multitude seek the ego scene
Whose twisted motives justify
Acts of pleasure based corruption
As though this monster left unborn
Would only live if they injected
Sins arrow to the Eros sky.

Along the chilled embankment lurks
A sinister yet saddening breed
Drawn more by hope than measured claw
Who stalk the drug infested streets,
Professional beggars with a tale
To half the affluent unprepared
Who might not miss that pound implored
Through misery or skilled deceit.

Yet what compares with Soho sleaze
Where many doorways hide a sin,
Those law bent clubs that sneer with guilt
As though one's life was meant to be
In lust entangled dingy bars
Or tread the stale, whore-haunted dark
The flip side of the London coin
That spins respectability

The Whole Slice

There was a time when sirens wailed
A fear struck warning to our hearts,
Yet some remained in sheltering tombs
As death and torture filled the skies,
Till docks and streets were rubble graves
With bodies strewn like old rag dolls,
And old class carriers flattened too
As London wept with blood stained eyes.

But there was something hidden deep
That we could never recognize,
This heritage that makes us one
Genetic force of unseen power,
Roman, Saxon, Dane and Norman
Unleashed from reserved deception
To rise in fury and defiance,
This flame that leapt in London's hour.

And when the smoke and dust had settled
Revealing shattered lives and homes
This unique inbred spirit's strength
Rose up to conquer misery
Never to forget nor wallow,
Till pride through hatred set her course
And from each district showed the nation
That London grasped her destiny.

So to tradition's celebration
Where nothing in the world compares,
Unison of will inspiring
Pageantry of natural taste and colour,
Horse guards and endless streams of forces
Filled the Mall and Square and Circus;
This is our right, though may it never
Be lost in Jingoistic valour.

Palace, museums and galleries
The endless sights of histories

Ivor Vernon Smith

Grown in the tourist culture bed,
They flood in awe from bus and train
From every country, race and creed
For this the mecca of their dreams
To stand, to see the aura bloom,
To just be there in pleasure's gain.

There under Nelson's watchful eye
A multitude of interest pass,
Where we at toil just blindly rush
And miss these treasures with our glance,
Could we but calm our City ways
Embrace the finest formed by man,
Though this would mean a slower tempo
To which our London could not dance.

I see the legends through the mist,
Holmes and Watson, Jekyll and Hyde,
And hear the footsteps in the fog;
Yet truth held terror worse than fiction
Through old Whitechapel's gas lit eyes,
Though countless were the brutish crimes
In secret lined those murky streets
That no wild thought dare lend prediction.

See the Fagins and the Dodgers
Covert and subtle with their aid
Sincerely bred from Dicken's day
Nourishing those gullible dreams
When all has faded but the hope
That London in her mighty pity
Would smile and lead away despair
To calm and nurture worn out schemes.

From Thornton Heath to Golders Green
And Stepney through to Wimbledon
We swing our compass to and fro,
Circular South, Circular North,

The Whole Slice

A one way maze of no return
Where Kamikaze taxis launch
On unsuspecting drivers' line
Lost in a labyrinth, back and forth.

Gone smog, white face, black handkerchief,
St. James's Park kissed fresh with Spring,
The Strand and Leicester Square are milling
Sweltering breathless as Summer yawns,
Trafalgar pigeons spread their mantle
A fountain backcloth sets the scene,
Oxford Street shoppers move as one
Though Autumn chills and Winter dawns.

Flanked by 'the corridors' down Whitehall
Carved greatness stonily peers around
The power surrounded Parliament Square,
Lords and Commons sealing our fate
As the Abbey sighs in stale respite
Whilst the Nation with suspicion grows
Wondering how their chosen champions
Earn salaries from dead debate.

Democracy her circle formed
Through forced convention led by Pitt
Turned in this city soft and stale
Yet through these halls time will release
True measure of our destiny
To live again our Empire glory
And resolutely plot our course
Avoiding wars and keeping peace.

Oval, Lords, Cup finals, Wimbledon,
Sports-orientation for all seasons
Adds to this wealth of atmosphere
Around the glittering clubs and bars,
Then to Theatre land world-envied
Supreme in cultured excellence,

Performances that touch the sky
And weave our memories round the stars

See the lovers' sun is setting
They own this moment on the bridge,
From Waterloo their stars are smiling
Around Westminster to St. Pauls,
Theirs is the gift that freedom earnt
When time has paused at London's leisure
Till chimes the hour across the Thames
And deep the City darkness falls.

Trade's commercial fierce momentum
Cares not for needed sacrifice
The price is paid yet never felt
For true perspective needs to pace
Itself and so relate the reason
Behind the unrelenting rhyme,
But London is what London does
And seldom sets the Marathon pace.

The multi-racial cards are dealt,
Kings and queens all crowned and vanished
The Jacks are trumps with Aces high
Upon the integrating day,
The clubs are full, the Diamonds rough,
The Hearts are lost the Spades have dug,
And should your stake increase with greed
You have to play the London way.

Yes, Dr. Johnson knew it then,
So only through exhaustion tire;
The rumbling, volcanic belly
That instigates this daily fight
Will with it's heart and mind erupt
Until the sparkling evening smiles,
And as you contemplate your day
Those London eyes will guide your night.

The Whole Slice

YOU ALONE HAVE HEARD

You alone have heard
The plaintive wail within your sleep
When apprehension's glinting dagger
Prods the psyche's under-belly
And stoic resistance fades
Before a withering consciousness
Reliving half forgotten dark, old times.
Fresh as dew on dusk's face
The moon-eyed night invades the still
And silent inspirations form
Brushing aside day-veiled inhibitions
Setting invention's alarm
To awaken spiritual aptitude
Sucked by flair's famished tongue
From creation's reluctant breast
Bloated with convention's non-vision,
Cough up the virus of restraint,
Clear well antibodies' word path
Through the limited fields of appreciation
Ignore grim furrows of influence
From stale critics' lost galaxy
Theirs are the stars that never guide,
Sleep the wild sleep that dreams allow
Listening to the unrepentant word
That you and you alone have heard.

9th July 1998

FROZEN CHEER

Why do I hear
Bells and laughter
A happiness cocktail stirred
By joy's numbed hand,
Now that I fear
Hell and after
Sorrow cannot be deferred
Nor heart withstand
The naked knife
Edging the time
Closer, deeper to the hour
Numbing reason
Heightening strife;
Nostalgia's rhyme
Turning blank verse meter sour
Out of season;
Kiss denying,
Mistletoe droops
Distant carols grace the air,
Others cheering,
Autumn dying
Her shoulder stoops
Heavy contrast worn with care
Pleasure fearing.

9th December 1996

OLD TWISTER

In the time it takes to read this line
A button is pressed
A city will fall.
Expedience has a new meaning,
Technological efficiency
Snaps its deliberate fingers,
Progress runs begging
The next historic move,
Taking up the slack to posterity.
What will they know, anyway,
Apart from what seems now
Compared with what seemed then,
Once it was all down to conditioning
Degrees, proportion etc.
But one day all will slip beyond the pale
Of rationality and compassion
As this old coil tries to out stare
The man-eyed hurricane
Sucked back to its lost beginnings.

31st July 1996

LINE OF DISTINCTION

Staring intent with boredom
Down suburbia's static streets
Of Spring's undrawn evening curtains
With lounge lit lethargy exposed
Where drained commuters wolfing their suppers
Crashed out, farting, tele-comatosed.

Why seek relief from apprehension
On the multi-stopping nightmare train
Down the dark line of distinction
That holds adventure and dismay,
A million untold stories lost
In the turmoil of a numbing day.

Drawn by this glib, magnetic city
On the fast and slippery track
Where slick honed capitalists lurk
And fresh rhetoric fruit is peeled;
Longing to stop and beat the trap,
Though communication cords are sealed.

Points and sleepers building rhythm
On the half forgotten problems
When technology's drug is shot
And the gold-spun web is weaved,
Intense or bored we stride worn platforms
Regardless of those means achieved.

Must we interrupt work for leisure,
How tolerant can this limbo be
When kissing arse is permanent
Company policy agenda
And no one dares to stand suspense
For the undropped shoe offender.

18th May 1998

OUR RHYME

There's a cluttered disposition
Ever striving for clarity.
Seldom to materialize,
It forms, shapes and fades
Returns in a different guise
Vanishing I confusion,
Ideals persevere in silent
An over determination looms
In a kaleidoscopic cacophony,
The strobe flickers in violence
Focusing another vision,
Numbness creeping like a dull ecstasy.
Kiss me into perspective, my love,
The experience in sin is past
Shelter my still belief
That we cling to our branch,
The last two leaves of Autumn.

Conjecture rules love's dark wave,
Let us bring some frantic order
To the clear motionless tide
Where infatuation's swollen ebb
Refuses to flow with our union;
Misspelling the right words,
Accentuating the wrong syllables,
Rhyming our blank verse.

9th October 1996

DRUNK'S ELEGY

Promise to miss the banquet
On a famished day
Tuck in the sheets for once
On another unmade bed
Just before you climb in,
Proud that you haven't been sick
As the stomach holds firm,
Like a hanging man's
Well-digested breakfast.
Living in the self convincing pit
Lying is part of the truth,
At least when discovered.
Turn forward the losing clock
The hour hand points to nothing
Endorsing an urgent second hand's
Futile movement to nowhere.
Before, now and after,
Nothing going space ward,
A drunken promise
To appease the moment.

22nd May 1996

SLEDGEHAMMER BLUES

With fifty working years behind you
Now explode with brash indignance!
What is achieved by your wasted time?
I cannot envy how you drift in space
Only the fact you have a choice.
You see, it's this morning ritual,
Having to reply 'shit'
To the nagging alarm clock.
When I am retired I will only set it once
When it goes off in the morning
I will hit it just once
With a fourteen pound sledge hammer,
Returning to a blissful slumber.

You however, already have this,
Your only real problem, my friend,
Is the degree of appreciation
That cocoons you from boredom's claw.
It appears the main responsibility
Lies within your existence
Of which you were hardly aware
During half a century of blinding toil.
Why sit in futile contemplation
Worrying about uncharged batteries
With no interests to justify lost time.
Celebration is not required behaviour
On the completion of labour's marathon.
Just think of me, one day, with that sledgehammer.

22nd July 1998

BOOMERANG

Was this held firm in genetic depths,
Honed perfection from intrinsic design
Released from inhibition's qualm
Erudition's hot words cooling,
Curving, swerving, spun unnerving
Across the arid plains of learning
Never to know interpretation
When once the grip that freed the flame
Enraged old age that stuck the page.

Or was it lust that threw the weapon
Blinding instinct-forming aim
That forged love's virginal
Sweet wages paid in memory's bank
Drawn, unrepaid, at highest interest
Spent through unrestraining dream work.
The boomerang so wildly thrown
Against day's unreturning light
Deflected only by the kill
Caught nonchalant, a hunter's right.

12th May 1998

SUMMER'S TORTURE

A day, Summer hewn
Climb the stifling, desperate noon
Persistent, inescapable
But for water drawn elixir
And Winter cool dreams.

Wiped sweat instantly returning,
Comfort killing, humidity's gasp
A bottomless cauldron
Boiled by a fire relentless
In its unbreathing pressure.

Leaden the germ bred air
Drawn by the quiet succumbing lung.
A respiratory nightmare lingers
In suffocating hysteria
Seeking escape to normality.

So the ice dream dawn is born
Yearning for a natural freshness
As fashion blind tanning fades
On Lemmings down a cancer cliff,
And an Autumn draught sweetly breathes.

21st August 1996

IF TEARS MUST FALL

If tears must fall
Let sadness nurture joy,
Far better free-expression
Than apathy's dull guise,
Yet live not for analysis
Nor caution's prop employ;
Flavour this feast of passion
With a pinch of compromise.

Hope deep, love heavy,
The bough of promise hung,
Mellow fruits of yearning
Took their final vow,
The sum of all intentions
Filled reality's tongue
Whilst a heaven's worth of blessing
Anoints devotion's brow.

Yet, if tears must fall
Remember this, my love,
When cynics mock and scorn
Emotional dreams,
They – merely touch a negative truth
Through fear-deflecting gloves;
You dance, forever fresh,
In freedom's clear and sparkling streams.

2003

ON MALTA

Gentle rock set firm in a Christian sea
Her fine edges roughened by foreign harm,
Sleep quiet from dark Ottoman memory
When Arabic and Romans' ruthless arm
Had been repelled with Islam hot for war.
A melting pot of warring factions stirred
On this vital Mediterranean shore,
Including blitz yet undescribed by word.

Black eyed, sandstone faces down scorched hills peered
Where once trod Paul and John's knights built and fought
Faith filled and poor the Maltese boat has steered
This ultimate escape their church has taught
Cross-drawn, falcon-spurred spirit brave released
With battles won, how keeps the natural peace?

13th September 1995

ON DREAMS

So what is a dream but a mystic leap
Repression of thought that spills from day
Where our untold scheme to conscious sleep
Speaks through the darkness that words cannot say.
When frustrations desire held pleasure's lie
Material dark from an unrehearsed script
Spat in truth's face yet could never deny
An audience who measured how far you slipped

No Freudian analysis need there be
No fantasy symbols' shades dark or light
For wishes fulfilled satisfactorily.
But reality's flashes sparked in the night.

Dreams are our uninhibited being,
Decision's freedom - our conscience fleeing.

9th January 1995

ON SICKNESS

Now sweet warmth of wellbeing vanishes,
Shadows of pain's infliction fill my brow
Though swift it may pass there is no time out now
As energy of health diminishes.
Sincere aid and sleep brings but scant respite
Through treatment of the symptom - not the cause,
Yet hiding from this knowledge, so to pause
And contemplate a long unequal fight.
I feel hell's deep fire through the shielding ice,
A dizzy sickness spreads the fever wild
No moderate suffering - cool or mild
But alone and stranded with cure's advice.
How soon, though, when this strength and nerve returns
Our memory loses that which once we yearned.

11th December 1994

Ivor Vernon Smith

PARANOIDEXPERTITIS

Running past the winning post
Never knowing that you've won
Not knowing when to stop
And concentrate on fun.

Turn about, my Jocko,
And kick your sporran high
Don't cry in your porridge
Why seek the hidden lie.

As you sing hymns, Taffy,
You choke on mountain air,
That coal dust in your veins
Was pumped without a care.

Jig and swear now, Paddy,
Fall blind upon the floor
Spit your brainless blarney
Why rub the worried sore.

Before our inward seeking
Contentment bred survival,
Now we set a blinkered course
Upon our non-arrival.

The largest empire ever,
Then the Commonwealth collapsed
Now experts on the fear of fear
Our policies have lapsed.

1st May 1996

PERHAPS IT'S JUST ME

Perhaps it's just me
Milking my grey day
Thriving on expectation
Of sympathy's comfort.
My life is at my nose,
All senses are touching
Terror rakes my chest,
Future devoid of perspective
Hangs on the moment,
Feet point no direction,
Lay-opinions meaningless,
Death sentence or reprieve.
The desperate hour draws close
Our reaper stalks the wards,
Frantic we work our shell
Ignorant of internal decay.
So what escapes my reason
In avoidance of our stress -
Why not drag us sooner
From this quicksand of agony.
Or perhaps it's just me.

14th February 1995

Ivor Vernon Smith

QUICK QUICK SLOW

When weakness in control concedes
In quiet debate to ponder.
A sweet retreat of unfelt wounds
And lets the mighty flounder,
For one spilt drop could multiply
To whip the floods tempestuous force
And turn a self-possessive eye
Upon an outward bending course.

How floats vain shallow victory,
No depth to drown uncoloured risk,
Come bathe a loser's sanctuary
Dwelling numb from ego's task,
Pierce presumptions bloated belly
Compulsion crammed in gaseous hell,
Contaminate youth's virgin folly
And influence raw, static will.

So lives the strength of unsound timing
It matters less than nerve can cay
That strips all reason from the rhyming
Leaving patience weakness free.
What cause is there to draw the flame
Rising scant above the coals,
What need to fan inferno's game
Burning quick fired unplayed roles.

14th January 1998

DISSERVICE

The worst disservice one can give
To fellowman or beast
Is bestowing credit
That is not due,
Clothing the naked ego
In a fool's cloak
Where huddled smug deception
Wallowing in numbed bliss
The recipient lives
A heaven's purgatory
Of hope-kissed clouds
From sun-denying gloom.

The best disservice one can give,
Which though it builds a pyre
Of unearned confidence
Burning those ashes to oblivion
With Hell's unrelenting fan,
Is a minimal scrap.

21st March 1996

A CHOICE?

When dying young and poor
Means all that's spared is pity
Then think how Keats, a Spring-rose plucked,
Left riches to posterity.

When living old and rich
Means quality we borrow
Then think of Ghetti, alone and lost,
Forgotten on the morrow.

When dying young and rich
Like butterflies in Summer flight
Never to know the mellow lull
Upon an Autumn night.

When living old and poor
Means that all is Winter long,
What would be a choice for mortals
If fate would share her hidden wrong.

17th January 1996

NEVER

Times never been
Sights never seen
Touch never felt
Thoughts never known
Kiss never touched
Heart never broke
Love never dreamt
Drive never spent
Hands never held
Fear never smelt
Breath never caught
Tears never fought
Cloud never swept
Pride never wept
Blind never shaped
Night never day
Aims never gained
Games never played
What never is
Is never this -

You never die!
I never lie!

28th February 1995

THE CUT

Shuffles my life-pack
Improves with practice
Becomes repetitive
Scrutinizes my style
Seeks a motive
Studies alternative

Relaxes with dexterity
Cheats for comfort
Raises the stake
Plays a losing hand
Smiles with fury
Dies from derision.

Deals from the bottom
Changes the deck
Borrows to lose
Cuts final pack
Wins in defeat
Returns to the night.

A PAWN GOES FORTH

I play you like a game of chess,
Often badly yet sincere
Endeavouring to keep ahead
Of your unforgiving move.
You decline my gambit
For sacrificing is all I know
Of giving, devoid of deceit.
Why do I open so strongly
Yet fade in my middle game
Watching my end begin -
A King of self-destruction.

So my Queen is lost
Through stalemate and perpetual check,
A pawn goes forth
To his ultimate objective
Reborn from obscurity
Where locked in unity
Defended his naked file
Assaulted by the Bishop's angle,
The rook's dimension
And the flexibility of knights,
Adjusting our plans, my love,
Crosschecked to a mating climax.

24th November 1994

Ivor Vernon Smith

DO I AWAKE?

Vanish you dreaded night
Where I have dreamt in spite
Of problems that expose
A deep division through sleep's eye,
Like vampires from the light.

Lie still my phantom heart,
Trembling spectre depart,
The rusty key turning
Opening my day-worn nerve box
Sun-primed for dawn's kick-start.

Hold fast my trembling sheet
Make lethargy defeat
The answering question
To repetition's aptitude
That drives my toil-bound feet.

Have I awoke to speak
Dark mind's perpetual leak
Or am I dumb to bear
Displacement's agony to drown
The scarred sore's turning cheek.

To never feel the thrust
That comfort will adjust
If to return to sleep
And never know what might reveal
From scraping of the rust.

31st October 1996

PRECOCIOUS DAWN

Precocious Dawn
Grates my still day
Reducing to fundamentals
Natural flavours of irony
Seasoned by a Winter's calm.
Time shits upon stale memory
The young forgetting to remember
The old remembering to forget,
Slaves to effects of convenience.
Breathe life my vacuum spirit
Into our infantile mergers
Scuff the frantic polish
Of our subtle innuendos,
Fair bullying to firm submission.

Hood the sterile sneer
That thrives on fads and whims,
Lead adult-ward infantile design
Along the fear-roughened kerb
Where the short-drop gutter beckons
Nudging them down when the cry rises.
Economy of kindness is an answer
To expectation of accolades
Make them savour every grain
Choking till their system groans,
Shakes out one fine thought
Painfully to a letter - a word -
Studies in sympathetic voice,
Whilst irony pauses to smile.

19th April 1995

AIR-SICK

When nature drags on
Tireless and deliberate,
I lie on the sun-side
Of mash potato clouds
On the blue gravy sky
Devouring in wonderment
Technological miracles
Of a blind layman day.

Turning up today's volume
On yesterday's radio
I touch the wavelength sound
Of well-tuned atmospherics.
A reluctant acceptance
Of the captain's tired assurance
As turbulent air pockets
Manifest themselves
Upon our frail deception.
A seat belt and watch adjustment,
Landing to relative logic
Through time's limbo lost or gained.

28*th* *September 1995*

TUMBRILS ARE RUMBLING

Tumbrils are rumbling
Down the pensive ward,
Apprehension bleeds prematurely
And breath-sucking heat
Dispels all escaping drowsiness
Centring vacant attention
On numbing existence.

A passing face lost in pre-med.
Smiles inwardly bravado's deceit
Echoing with stale clichés
Of layman-dumb reassurance
Vanishing down the blue blanket avenue
To an unseen, unheard world
Of masks and anaesthesia.

Half past two, you're due at three
Thoughts reduced to mundane glimpses
Pre-med playing its box of tricks
Sense replaced by spurious drivel
A safety curtain on fear's last act.
Tumbrils are rumbling,
Your debut with silence begins.

3rd April 1995

Ivor Vernon Smith

HEADS OR TAILS?

Why have we to win with words,
Determination's shallow victory,
Let us lay down an embargo or speech
And think out our war in silence.
Night's simmering star-spell lingers
On gospel wizard breath
A thinking creed's sermon of dream
Chews tastefully on a hidden truth
Exempt the testing of patient fist
Or stifling of boredom's yawn.

Why have we to lose with deeds
Attacking defences, defending attacks
Wronging our rights, righting our wrongs
A Greek tragedy or tragic Greek
Jewish fault or faithful Jews
The motive justice or justice motivated.

Ingredients boil in diverse ways
Lost in fastidious preparation
A tongue or limb holds court
We balance on the scales of greed.

11th October 1995

SPARK

Flickering brief
But never to die
Posterity smiling
Upon a fragile urge
That seemed so little
With which to be parted
At a frantic time
When stress-coloured,
Flair formed fragments
Split infinity's atom.
Over mundane antiquity
An insidious dust cloud hung
Choking inventive ways
Whilst the nodding man
From time-trodden establishment
Smiled with his y yellow teeth
In his downhill routine.

Our motive is missing
Our engine is blown
We are left with the hissing
A perpetual groan
On our spark we are pissing -
And the magic is flown.

16th May 1995

DARK FORM OR ESSENCE

Dark form or essence
Fair shape or charm
Symmetry mellows

Roughness in calm;
Sun-held, sky-watched
The sea-shaping earth
Draws on breath's appetite
Grips bloated girth

Web of disease
Triangular spun
Passing the ghost
From father to son.
Wasted dark moments
Slackened the screw
Love knows no measure
To tighten the view.

Dark form or essence
Fair shape or charm
Heart pointing finger
Mind bending arm.

5*th* July 1995

A CHILD'S NIGHT OUT

Yet one more evening of endurance
Standing firm as a child
Outside the Edlin's bar
With a giant biscuit
And a pint of lemonade,
Inside came strange raucous sounds
A cacophony of shouts and laughter
The door swung wide enough
To glimpse a smoke-filled mystique
And a ringing till, crowd hidden,
Always the jabber on unlistening ears
A smell of stale beer decadence,
Defiant singing to an out of tune honkytonk,
Foul names hurled with whisky breath.

The east wind ripped down Ship Street
Tearing at my short trousered legs
As parents walk by with children
Towards the beckoning seafront,
Where a welcoming promenade
Basks in a different world.

And I, chained to a pub doorway
Never knew if it was meant to change.
A child's brick-blocks of resentment
Built on the stopped clock of patience.

14th June 1995

VESUVIUS DAY

Demons heard with a naïve ear
Devoid of listening sieve,
There's a paranoid displacement
Spilling and sticking, underwatched
Like the burnt milk syndrome
On over-ripe impression
Compulsion's eruption bursts forth
An overflow of jealousy and vengeance
Clogging the psyche, blinding the heart
Onward to the passive plain
That knew nothing but a tideless sea
Complacent in its tidy shoreline.

Lust's lava ever returning to its task
Pride blistering cheeks ego scarlet
In unrequiting passion, a death thrilled climax
Succumbing through ultimate compulsion
To consummate a lifetime's need
Burying deep all moral conscience.

How strange the lush green offspring forms
From destruction's mighty penis
Untouched by love's ecstatic purpose
As though the lungs of hell exploded
On fate's unsuspecting innocence,
Breathing carnage on a Roman day.

18th October 1994

NARROW PRAYER

A narrow will poised
On the ethical tightrope.
Conscience taut
Beyond flexibility
Unbending in judgement
Cramped visionless
In static posture.

Let us pray, my love,
Beyond the rational pale,
Pride her brittle spine
Is breaking to the strain
Snapping like an oak's resistance
Weak with strength,
The frail bamboo bending
Strength from weakness
As the tumult rages
Then abates to find
The towering reed
Above the fallen King.

The moral treadmill grinds
From grain to dust
Sweeping right's wrong
Down the narrow path
Far from the unformed bread.

10th November 1994

Ivor Vernon Smith

IF THERE IS A POINT

I wonder if there is a point
In convincing people of the obvious
Through glimpses or by labouring;
Perhaps there is, if only to convince oneself.

Religion seems a certain non-starter
Concepts drifting to abstract oblivion,
Politics lost in endless tub-thumping,
Air-punching ideals cliché-hammered.

I wonder if there is a point
In working through a torrid day
On a treadmill of promises,
Insults repetition and falsehoods.

Socializing is a tiresome spirit
A witless energy for escapism;
Nothing seems worth anything now,
The circus ends with or without me.

I wonder if there is a point
Talking sense at this moment,
Who will remember anyway
Or is it only ourselves we impress.

In a perfect dream there is perfect truth
It is only reality that lies
For sleep wears no imposters hat,
Perhaps there is a point - who knows.

3rd *May 1994*

AGNOSTIC EYE

Holds a turning mirror
Revolving a static plot
Barely glimpsed yet seen
As an unclear denunciation;
A questioning nomad
Seeking all, believing none,
Watering a mystery's
Miracle-worth of dreams.

Spin the wheel wildly
Let the lottery commence
Loading stake on an unseen choice,
A premium parable bled
On sermons' sales pitched in goodness
Where heart-propped conscience beats
In time to ritual tremors
Tone deaf to the blinding monotone.

How grips the outstretched hand
Is it fist or greeting,
Honesty or honed routine,
Damnation's threat or invitation -
White the ecclesiastic knuckles
Pulpit -thumping fear and hope
Into a sinner's church-dayed asylum
Slamming Hell's unhinged door ajar,

And through that gap we witness
Chosen testaments in compulsion's word -
The mystic old, the cryptic new,
The Moses dream, the Jesus scheme
Holding back the dawn of righteousness
As generations fill the stage
And an audience of souls applaud

In silence. God in man's image.

Blind the heathen eye reveals
The inner nothingness of loss being,
Shadows within hidden darkness
Descend hell's infinite maelstrom
Living endless pain of disbelief
Stifled deep in barriers of existence
Untouched, unfeeling, unknowing,
Cocooned in day less eclipse.

Deceit her opium mind addicts
Unshelled a Judas double-cross,
A many shaded smile concealing
Hypocrisy's tangled path
As though the following of each creed
Saw hallmarks of a beauteous truth
When deep in sly entanglement
Lost insidious mystics lurk.

If preaching draws upon the good
In genuine form less prejudice
Then essence can be justified
For all this thumping of the Word,
Yet could the opposite apply
In non-believing bias
And that ingredients of the font
Create unproven testament.

This war in blood stirs endlessly
Congealing to a pagan mire
And though the signposts point for truth
What makes that crossroad choice
Which commitment fills the spirit
Holds the uncut key designed
When closer to this sightless knowledge
Peers the calm agnostic eye.

15th August 1994

GAMES

There's many a rule that can apply
To any problem you can name
But whether you're shot in the foot or the eye
Its knowing how well to play the game.

The persistency of nature's law
Shows consistency's perfect lie,
And though your stroke be deadly poor
Seeks integrity's alibi.

Darkness hides a sinister course
Where the ghost of winning haunts,
And though a hell-whipped driven force
Blinds all, inspiring are the taunts.

Equality lines up for the start
Pros and cons the ideal race
But on the first bend loses heart
And on the home strait loses face.

What real triumph have we here
Where gods and devils hold the sway,
Expectancy, hope or chosen fear
Are all lost in a future day.

And so these rules that do apply
To problems, success and grandiose schemes,
Mean nothing lest they justify
The discipline destroying dreams.

14th June 1994

THE HAUNTER OF MY DARKEST SLEEP

The haunter of my darkest sleep
Has lain within his coil
In spiralled honesty, where dread's
Obscure translation has warmed for me
A bower deeper than this
My shallow heart has known
Or from which my tainted spirit
Ever will succumb.

Day's matter has skipped before my sight
As a thought-wind driving cloud-words
Across the sun's reason,
And though this bed the pleasure
Holds scant remorse
There is for me the clammy dawn
That grips the sky and sees the wind
And steals my memory's treasure.

The taunter of my lightest hour
Has scoffed each deepening line
Delivered through this throbbing skull
With no redeeming lie;
And so I flee the murmuring copse
Afar to the forest's spring
And bathe in the sunlit stars' cascade
Where the nightly rebels sing.

29th March 1976

Ivor Vernon Smith

NEGLECT

Another racist day dawns,
For everyone its white honky
Or black bastard time,
Paki bashing, Indian untouchables,
The prejudiced fur flies
No exemptions, its hate and shit,
But worse - sincere hypocrisy,
Abuse me, insult my parentage
But for god's sake cut the crap
With that patronising smile,
The reassuring hug
And the calm gentle nodding.
Kick my lily-white arse
Tar and feather my ideals,
Ridiculing principles
With lavatorial innuendoes
But be faithfully honest
And admit there is a difference!

It isn't just colour or creed,
Culture, religion or bias,
Birthright, dress or cuisine,
Mentality or attitude,
Civilisation, deprivation,
It's not just that which guarantees
This unbridgeable gulf.
No. Its neglect of continuity -
Nothing works nor ever will
Unless durable beyond all fault,
Not through indoctrination
By will or conditioning

It has to be natural, fluid
Beyond all self-convincing thought,

But sadly it is less than this
Our victorious march will lead us
To yet another defeat
Night will shed her silent tears
Upon the drum of discrimination
And another racist day will dawn
Things will only be what they seem
For man was never meant to learn!

CHINESE WHISPERS

In that covert circle
Lives a perfect message
Passed in muted confidence
Still mind -linked
Oblivious of the subtle change
With meaning or intimation,
A syllable's faint deformation
Insulting integrity of context
Yet lost in enthused belief.
Onwards drifts the secret word
Onward genuine passing of thought
Opening passive ears'
Worldwide naivety,
Trusted agent in continuity.

Twilight's day losing breath
Inhales returning stars' aroma
Of glittering galaxy's vision
Spinning an endless truth
Upon a dark earth's muddled brow;
Then forms the game's enigma
A Chinese whispered sincerity
Living its early promise
Endorsing its hidden vow,
Till up-geared the turning
Leaps to avoid spun climax
Deluding the psyche's intention,
Diluting spirit with fantasy
A watered down opinion's worth.

23rd *August 1994*

MARRIED BLISS?

Is it chemistry
Sealing a bond,
Does another row
Strengthen the unity,
If so why not row
Continuously, for ever
During lovemaking,
Nagging each other to sleep
Following out dreams
To that first awakening moment.

No! By all means
Clear out the surplus shit
From old relationships
Dig out stagnation's ash
With a perfect care
Re-kindling those embers
That form the flame
From part to whole.
Unique ingredients
Guarded with sweet possessiveness.

12th May 1994

Ivor Vernon Smith

THE DAY OF THE SALESMAN

Commercialised syrup thickly spread
Across the bread of gullibility;
This is the plan, boy;
Bolt it down without a thought-wasting chew
You need a quick lining for the big heave;
These guys could have blinded Hitler with schmaltz
And convince China the third world was doomed
Long before they were breathing in earnest.

I never imagined a daisy field with barley borders
And a harvest of fly-filled buttercups,
Neither could you;
None of us knew how to piss up the wind before
And smell of jasmine from the spray,
Wallowing in dysentery's relief
In the media orientating of the shittened leg.

We thought once (long before they won)
On a still day when the mellow air sighed
With the genuine prospect of its worth,
When experience spoke without the planted word
Before the poles were joined in grasping seams.
We thought once (long before they came)
Of the moment, and of being,
This will never return, it was never meant to be!
Sorry, son, I never meant this for you
Somewhere I got lost in the syrup,
It tasted beautiful at first
Till my brain grew sweet and soft
And I was never meant to remember.
Now I need them as they need me
To help them forget the days of the cold sell.

10th December 1980

ON FRIENDSHIP

Judge not true friendship
By conversational flow
But by the ease
When silence tends to grow.

Dispel all inhibition
From each derisive word
Lost in freedom's company
Like spring forever stirred.

Beware incipient flames
That through time's chimney leap,
Rekindle afterglow with care
And fan with patience deep.

THE UNFINISHED SUPPER

Grief-sore frantic the blind heel dug
Hard upon sanity's softening flank;
Frothingly steam-eyed
Of demon spite
Boldly the yawning steed of progress
Ventured from the blood-spun whip
Relentless in a supper-carving spree;
So ever changing pace and step
Performing neat formality's dressage.

So as one the crowd of muscles leapt
Flexing hope as a steel-tongued goddess
Tempting love as in Atlanta's race;
For in youth's loins, libido simmering,
Procreations deep compulsion lurks
Savouring a jealous twin to goodness,
Whilst blind hells hymen yields her sin
And waits atonement, purpose-doomed.

Grief-sore frantic still the blind hill dug
Now numb to vomit-trodden wine,
For who does feel the nausea in hell's grape
When treads the foot on anger bent;
In haste the bread is broken to death's crumb
And of this crumb is caught the soul's digestion,
And this the night's repast lies heavy yet
To choke in conscience on the loaf-sick heart.
Foreboding's cough barks hollow on the dusk
Freed briefly from the hacking lungs of day,
And softly do the candle stars being to play
Upon those tapestries of patient queens
Whose spouses died long ere the ghost willed truth
Had passed beyond those tarnished lips,
As fragile grew the necks beneath the passive crown

Whilst cause and certainty were banished to the tomb

And though morose and wan through agitation
The sadness leaping 'cross the death-like face,
The sperm of fate bends forth upon a shapeless world
Treating dying breath as though it were conception formed;
The sin of wisdom knows little yet the mirror's face
But surely feels the knife and fork upon the flesh of time,
Till when the revelry begins and twilight fancies grow
A multitude of serpents hangs heavy on the pensive air

Interminable the late repast this night,
How slowly do the festering vessels flow
Throughout the serpent-gloom's entangled trauma,
Whilst there reined taut within hysteria's grip
This blasé appetite is lost though novelty serves on;
Unfinished this supper for all mankind
Lavishing season salt upon an unhealing year;
As grief-sore frantic the blind heel dug.

WEDDING SPEECH

Apprehension's knife piercing,
Faking interest in food and company
As conversation bubbles,
Attention, magnetic drawn,
To a white laced perfection
Swimmingly adjusting to a dream-dayed passing;
The groom, grinning off apprehension
Of the ultimate spotlight.
Yet it's you with a spoon-tinkling glass
Fixing a multitude of eyes,
Stilling wine loosened tongues
For the silence you alone must fill.
Suddenly children are parentless
Running amok through chairs
With an infectious madness
Clashing with your feeble attempt to impress.
'Shut up you little bastards', I smile quietly,
Hoping to gain a little sympathy
For my inarticulate mutterings.
Unprepared - thought I'd be clever,
Sod it - forgot half already
Apart from some inane anecdote
About a childhood trip that went wrong
Poorly delivered in giggling embarrassment
Which seemed to blend aptly
With the childrens' maniacal shrieks
And the squeaking chairs of a hundred numbed arses.
At last a toast, absent friends etc.,
Relieved, half-hearted applause
Followed by neurotic doubts
Of video exposure for posterity.

25th *October 1994*

Ivor Vernon Smith

BEING

Did we hold hands till sunset
Feeling time but not the hours,
Ungoverned by aspiration
Essence or destiny.
Kiss the stars for me, my love,
I will never reach your heights,
Be caressed by that meridian spell
In which you alone exist.
I could not bear you in my dreams -
Being the nadir of my despair
Awakening and finding you not there;
Let me enjoy reality's tears,
Each time we part death smiles
Yet in limbo to my being,
A borrowed death soon repaid,
When I am reborn on the morrow -
A lifetime's absence overstayed.

Did we breathe in unison
Reaching peaks of our endeavour
From a mire of despondency,
Not knowing, feeling, caring
If we were stepping out or in
Providing we were one - uninspired
Flowing like a hidden cataract
A jungle's eternal secret
Caressing in the fresh, cool foliage
Our minds and bodies trembling
In the definitive ecstasy of being.

We turn and turn about - lost
Yet found within our inner self
Thankful for frustrion's eruption
Bursting forth in tears of blood

Down yesterday's tired cheeks, parched,
Congealing love's magnetic cells.

Did we hold hands till sunset
Till a Venus eye shone her blessing
And a corny old moon performed
Forming a backcloth cliché
To our unrehearsed opening night.
We kissed; the earth was on hold
Every fibre of our being gel
With cherished fulfilment
Lost in Kismet's sweet design
What care we of fool's existence
A lightning fork could never part
We are the storm in passion's plot
The calm beyond the weeping rain;
Love me! endure me! haunt me forever!
Your joy and misery are mine
Through space, time and infinity -
Together as fate's intention.

7th December 1994

LOGICAL BOLLOCKS

Logical Bollocks
Is at it again
It knows what it knows
But cannot refrain
From thinking too loudly
Two dimensional crap
Which valid opinion
Would not even tap.

Into the dead night
Blind, witless and stark
Out of a warm bed
To piss in the dark
Aiming with fervour
At the still waiting pan
Not feeling one moment
From where it began.

Out on the chessboard
Where nothing is heard
Pieces in silence
Obey without word
Where caution is followed
And gambits declined
A plot has emerged
Which logic defined.
Logical bollocks
In haste to express
Knowledge of nothing
Yourself to impress,
Allow time for fault
When others may mock
Whilst in the interim
Quick thought can take stock

Ivor Vernon Smith

4th April 1995

MIND OF DESPAIR

This mind that is within my head,
But which I know I'll never own
This mind where torment dwells,
To veil the thoughts I've never known.

What are these depths in which my spirit lies
Enshrouded always by fears and dreads,
That eclipses love and precious ideal
And tears my confidence to shreds.

When does the tumult cease
That does cause this pang within my breast,
This doom to which I clasp myself
Unwittingly entwined in branch and nest.

Sailing the ocean of unfathomable depths,
The sea of life with waters troubled,
To sink with aspirations vanished,
No matter whether efforts doubled.

The nightingale sings his evensong
Such few cares on which to contemplate,
Except the unforeseen enemy which swoops,
For who is master of his fate?

What would I give to extend my hand
And clutch the dreams I had in youth,
To relive those longings, hopes and doubts,
Without the knowledge of the truth.

This weakening drug to which I succumb
Wondrous daydreams filled with perception,
Till waking, startled from my reverie,
I discover it's a fool's deception.

To concentrate without a furrowed brow,
Would be a feat when filled with sorrow,
Reluctant for the arms of Morpheus,
Ever afraid of black tomorrow.

Yearning to appreciate once more
The taste of wine and fragrance of a rose,
A song, a joke, a baby's look,
This agony of mine that no one knows.

Now heavy-legged with no facade,
In distant fields I hear a bell
And this short walk is all but o'er
As louder, louder grows the knell!

22nd October 1973

BUFFER

There is an acceptance
On all good behaviour
Being normal and expected,
A philanthropic norm
Shedding winter's tired skin
On the untamed spring.
There is encouragement
For all forms of goodness -
Spontaneous and sublime;
Let's fire our Samaritan arrows
From a green-dawn bidding
Forming a clouded nourishment
Around an unrepentant sun,
Burning deep sincerity's wish
Upon a beholdent cross
With perfection's iron
Etching a memory's debt.

There is a judgement
That exceeds consummate need,
Blasts conscience to infinity,
Spits a world drowning sea
From an unstudied throat
Sadistic motive, spite driven,
Shredding a willing flesh
To its marrowless bone,
Spinning a pointless top to death,

There is a resistance
Against which there is no dream
No power of imagination,
Just no acceptance
Through idealistic hope
That one day there is a buffer

Absorbing all goodness and reason
Enduring and omnipotent,
So that we feel the calming waves
Caress our savage bodies
In unconditional warmth

Acceptance, Judgement, Resistance -
The whole compromising conflict.

THE BALLAD OF MELINDA GREY

One day there was a time between
The failing twilight to a dream
Where shadowed images were screened,

That dance upon the memory's bank
And swirl to a hazy lilting theme
Down rutted tracks that corn fields flank,

And though the wind of mystery blows,
Her gossamer profusion veiled,
I see how at the heart she goes,

For as she whips the sea of grain
I sadly see that smile death-paled
Against the tempest's timeless pain.

The smile she bore meant for no other,
Was ever mine though life would hinder
And would in passing briefly smother,

The eyes and mouth which love did form
So to become my sweet Melinda
And float within each reverie's dawn.

She glides upon a stallion grey
Thundering across the starlit vale;
Her hair a flaxen mantle lay

Upon the swan-like shoulders bare
And there so poised and beauteous pale
She rode till dawn with not a care.

The sun it's cloak of gold did spread
Across the dew-kissed slumbering Weald,

Toward this she turned the stallion's head

But he with mane a'bristling reared
As though a demon in him filled,
Then swift toward the Dyke he steered

And then there came a motley crowd
All chanting through the dawning still
To gather as a hill-top shroud,

Then all as one they turned her way
So she could not pass at her will,
And tore her from that stallion grey.

"How ride thee fearless though the night"
They cried "And to this spot appeared."
"I know not, but my steed took fright

And bore me to this awesome place
For we were Ditchling bound but steered
As though the devil in him raced."

"Possessed therefore, thou wanton bitch!"
They screamed, and ducked her deep, but she
Survived, so making her a Satan Witch.

The hill-top staked with deadly lust
Not heeding any frantic plea
To burn her innocence to dust

Now when I gaze upon the weald
And fierce the wind blows long-grass tides
As Autumn sighs o'er Summer yield,

I hear her whispering soul once more
Across the Sussex countryside
That nags upon the festering sore.

So now I seek the time between
The failing twilight to a dream
Where shadowed images are screened

That dance upon the memory's bank
And swirl to a hazy lilting theme
Down rutted tracks that cornfields flank.

19th December 1979

MIRROR

There's a certain comfort
Eating my shit sandwich
Cocooned with insecurity,
Pockets lined with credit,
No one expects much
Certainly no more than they get,
The minimum of expectancy
That's it - so tough shit
If you wish to expand my world,
So why try to infect me
With your ideals and aspirations.,
Let me dig my own footings
Who cares if the lot collapses
It's my mess - so leave it!

Let's take it all out of context
Lose our perspective
Loosen our safety belts
We don't need to brake
Sooner or later we'll hit something
Then all meaning will begin
As our mirror rushes up
Polished clean of bravado.

2nd *June 1994*

EL MONTGO

I first saw you, El Montgo,
Scanning fertile plain so proud
With an ever changing hue
Touching earth and sea and cloud,
Sweet drug of tranquillity
Far from turmoil's frantic crowd.

I gaze at you, El Montgo,
As your face reflects the dawn,
Green cheeks blend to golden grey
And each day I feel reborn
With this comfort in your presence
Should my hopes appear forlorn.

I think of you, El Montgo,
Filling space since time began
Absorbing generations
With mighty memory span;
Hushed are mountaintops around
With some untold mystic plan.

I turn from you, El Montgo,
To the valley in the night
And feel that stars below me
Are each life's inspiring light,
And when the moon is fading
Deeper vision holds delight.

I shall return, El Montgo,
To re-acquaint this pleasure
And lie in bliss to contemplate
Your riches at my leisure,
We are as one, El Montgo -
You are my Spanish treasure!

28th September 1994

MINOR KEY

Mellow tone -
Notes lingering on,
Illusion's kiss
Melting star wards
Sky building
A memory's future,
Only night's canopy
Remaining constant,
All else changing
With forgotten music,
Love's thoughts gel
Like a pensive chord
Blending the senses as one
Spiralling down to you, my love,
A magnet of search
Upon devotion
Drawn from each as one
Caressing the minor key
As moonlight veils
The nightingale's crescendo,
Filling nostalgia's dream
In sweet escape.

Ivor Vernon Smith

INDECISION

A hiccup lost to destiny
Taking flight on hysteria's wing
Fuelled indefinitely by paranoid despair
On the final frontier of confidence.

A stuttering mystery yawning
In stark disbelief at reality
Spills untidy words on the grey hill
Obliterating a pensive sun.

Over-determination holds
Fear's key to a mystic lock
Turning unsteadily, yet sure
A further mystery awaits.

A cough destroys the silence
In conflict with the throat's intent,
Echoes from the passive walls
Holds a nervous court to ransom.

A faltering movement lingers,
Stumbles before the changing wind
Farts free sweet wisdom's perfect breath
Receives in full a pissed relief.

Turns the smiling cheek away
Revealing insincerities lie,
Turns and changes in lost decision
As the unrelenting world spins by.

25th July 1994

SLANG

How quickly modern terms
Develop into clichéd crap,
Revealing nothing but the time
And where you are upon the map.

Stupid methods, sillier words
Try to encapsulate our days
When nothing is more dated
Than these jargon loaded ways.

What's in abbreviation
Or a slick and sharp retort,
Just a mere acceleration
With no quality of thought.

Americans need a slanging prop
For them true English is a waste,
If it's quick it's good and why not -
They're culture blind in worst of taste.

We have no need to follow them
With their tacky verbal muck,
Perhaps some context swearing
With an Anglo-Saxon 'fuck!'

Latin Greek and Roman
The basis of our tongue,
There's quite sufficient wording
On that highest language rung.

4th October 1994

I TOUCHED THE SADNESS THERE

I touched the sadness there
Upon those tender eyes,
That so beguiled my reverie,
That held my muted sighs.

I kissed the hidden smile,
Those lips of bitten pride,
How could I ever know the grief
Her infant spirit cried.

I lived that moment long
That fed my groping heart,
How could I ever miss a father's love,
We were a death apart.

I passed upon my way
Never to share the sorrow,
When she could never clasp once more
That hand upon the morrow.

SCARLET GREY

Bedlam is the poet's dread
In kaleidoscopic sound
Led boldly in a shrill array
Where sound and vision merge
And all is scarlet grey.

And through the mottled vision drifts
The swirling hope of ethereal bliss
Thwarted ever by the open ear
Rising with the drowning wind
Panting chosen gusts of fear

But what is sight and sound this night,
This reverie which numbs the pen
Yet fades within the dulling air
Compared to this romantic plight,
Love's unrequited, fervent prayer.

For in the poet's mind lay bare
Those nerve ends tattered from the fray,
And sleep holds scant respite nor strength
To lend in dreams of sweet solace
Such agony of endless length.

Ivor Vernon Smith

A DEEPER AUTHORITY

How doomed the natural day,
A silhouette against the tiring hills
Of etiquette and protocol
Of man- made climes and attitudes
Which lurked from vales of pride
Where stark concern drew on fate's mist
And sucked love's cataract dry.

There boomed the echoing sound
Across the poles where lovers lay
But they were numb to hear
The skull-dry waves that crashed upon their tomb
And dumb to see the narrowing gap
'Twixt poles and reason poles and day
To feel the night worms drilling at their sap.

Here groomed sin's fashioned lie,
Nurtured flints from the ruins of youth,
A deeper authority shadowing the naked thigh
That breathed in sly betrayal's looser flesh
And sold an endless heaven frozen psalms
Weaving graphs in star-lined platitudes;
Now see dawn's spectre raise her cancerous arms.

26th April 1976

IMPASSE

Morality fills the air,
Heart-felt platitudes
Spill undiluted fairness
Upon the cynic's arid ground,
Mystic shadows lengthen
On the grey syndrome day
And endless pails of words
Lowered down an empty well
Return enriched with shallow splendour
Spreading a thin layered justice
Upon love's converted wisdom.

Legality kills the air,
Impassive the plumb-lined eye
Throws a daggered stare
Upon all due process,
Spills not compassions tears
Down unrelenting paths,
As the gathered water boils
A callous steamed crescendo,
Leaving but a vapour of despair
Incomprehensibly bland
Permanent in its scalded blemish.

Justice hides her head -
Conjecture-manacled,
Locked in heart-mind limbo
Patiently devoid of spite
Of prejudice and hate
Waiting for law's perfect key.

5th May 1994

Ivor Vernon Smith

WHAT DOES IT MATTER

I wonder if future generations
Will remember much about us
And our throwaway ideals,
Our degenerate pastimes
Dressed up in compassion's mystique,
Civil rights, animal rights,
Gay liberation, child psychology
And the abolition of hanging.
Something had to give
The candle burnt in the middle
And endless washing in a dirty bath
With a vanishing soap
On a germ infested flannel;
The scum plimsoll line rose,
Below was safety's squalor
Above was pointless aspiration.

The air pungent with unearnt liberty
Smelt pure to the untrained nose.
Perhaps we worked too hard at misery
filthy with credit
When spending didn't hurt
Bringing the future forward
With a conditioned impatience.

Still we must have wondered at our parents
With weekly trips to pawnbrokers,
No television and a cats whisker wireless,
Bread and dripping for tea,
Then talking a load of crap up the pub,
They had a war to sort them out though
And something to rebuild afterwards.

Still if you don't want to be remembered

Just fade into another forgotten sunset.

11th May 1994

NOWHERE

Let us all rush -
To nowhere,
It is the only place
That makes any sense,
As spirits sink constantly -
In nowhere,
We will all know
Where we are or were
For the first time -
At nowhere,
For no one knows
Where they are meant to be
Past, present or future -
Till nowhere,
Do we make sense
For ourselves or others
In reaching goals -
Of nowhere,
Truth and lies merge
Living is dying,
Joy finds despair -
From nowhere,
But boredom is bliss
And stress is the norm,
Just an illusion -
With nowhere,
Wonderment dawns
Misery yawns,
Happy in shit
And nowhere!

16th May 1994

LOVE'S HABIT LOST

Habit formed in numbed belief,
The norm for pleasure - blinding reason
Leaves nothing for the will's resistance
Which knows but little stark relief
From loyalty to a plotted treason -
Brings sin's mile to touching distance.

No parasol beneath the sun
Nor cover from the violent storm
Dark elements they hold the stake,
A weather's wind throws everyone,
Deceiving all with fresh or warm
Till suddenly its freeze or bake.

'Amoral,' drones the first excuse -
A cliché plea in self-defence,
'Sustained', agrees the judge's sleep,
'For juries we've no further use -
This word has proved there's no offence,
Dismiss! A counsel's legal leap!

City of bowler hatted Crombies
Passing through the evening dust,
Lost deep in apprehensive strain;
Wearily homeward uniformed zombies.
Fawning daily in salaried trust
Praying for their sardine train.

What is this tune we seem to hear
Casting aura of infinite charm
In listening habit so to learn,
Melt's frozen apathy to a tear
Cocoon's the memory from harm
Yet allows emotion to discern.

Ivor Vernon Smith

SCRUFFS

What's in this dressing down?
Concertina jeans, screwed up tee shirts
Shin length tongued trainers
Forming a designer-torn mess.

Pass the dummies' watching window
Drags a scarecrow army
Numb to posterity's disbelief
A chrysalis cocooned
From the world's shit
Plotting their own destruction.

The inner vision of discovery
Haunts their belong,
Nullifies their being,
An organized roaming
Defiant in a sloppy perfection,
The product of our careless loins' delight.
Or are they gods in dirty shirts
Preaching to their own existence.

We flush in the dark
The cistern groans.

8th November 1994

About the Author

Ivor Smith was born in London in 1935 and the family moved to Brighton at the beginning of the war.

He eventually returned to live in London at the age of 20 where he met and married Shirley, a London girl. They rented a flat in Streatham South London and eventually moved to Rochester in Kent where they raised their three children.

He has been writing poetry for forty five years, mainly at night but because he was a self-employed hairdresser he was able to write at work when the opportunity arose.

Printed in Great Britain
by Amazon